DERRY

with Michael McMullan

PUBLISHED BY HERO BOOKS
LUCAN
CO. DUBLIN
IRELAND

Hero Books is an imprint of Umbrella Publishing
First Published 2023

Copyright © Michael McMullan 2023
All rights reserved

A CIP record for this book is available from the British Library

Cover design and formatting: jessica@viitaladesign.com
Photographs: Sportsfile, Derry Journal, Mary K Burke, Danny O'Kane and Ciaran McNally

★ DEDICATION ★

To my late father-in-law, Patsy Kennedy
and his late brother, Mickey

They would have fairly enjoyed the stories on these pages

★ CONTENTS ★

★ ACKNOWLEDGEMENTS ★

FIRST OF ALL, and most importantly, I want to say a special word of thanks to my wife, Pauline. Without her support and encouragement, I'd never have got this project off the ground.

A book was something I always dreamt of writing and when Liam Hayes floated the idea in the middle of a busy year, it was Pauline who convinced me to give it a go. In the weeks and months since, she has been an unbelievable support with the 'just keep at it' and 'you're nearly there' statements. Plus, she is the world's best proof-reader.

To our daughter, Erin, I'd like to thank you for your patience as I worked on this. Thanks also for your interest in how the chapters developed, and I apologise for the hours spent in the office at home trying to get the stories on these pages pulled together.

During lockdown, Erin began to write a wee story of her own and has threatened to get back to it… and become Derry's answer to JK Rowling. Why not?

I would like to sincerely thank my parents, Mickey and Sally, for everything they have done to support me over the years, and for planting and nourishing the seed for my love of the GAA. They trucked me to training when I was younger and took me all across Ireland to watch Derry. Never mind the mountains of jerseys over the years.

I remember standing on top of an icebox in Clones to peek over the heads of the crowd on the old grassy hill as Derry won the Ulster minor title in 1989. Daddy took me to Croke Park for my first All-Ireland final later that year, when we won the All-Ireland minor title. They always took a great interest in my playing days and this has continued since I started writing about the GAA. Over the past two years, they have travelled with us to many of Derry's games, and all the performances were fully dissected by the time we'd get home.

Thanks a million. These words don't come close to doing justice for everything you have done for me.

I am particularly pleased for them that Chrissy McKaigue mentioned my brother, Antóin in his chosen game – Slaughtneil's win over St Vincent's. His save in Páirc Esler that day was one of those proud 'big brother' moments after spending time coaching him at underage.

I also have to thank my in-laws, the Kennedy family from Ballinascreen, for all their support and interest in my sports reporting and writing. The first time I met Pauline's father, Patsy, back in the 90s, we talked football, and we continued to do so until his sad passing at Christmas 2022. An encyclopaedia of a man. He was deep in my thoughts as I put the book together. While it's extremely sad he won't get a chance to read the final product, he was a huge motivation for everything that appears in these pages. When I told him I was starting off the book, he took a great interest. It's an honour to dedicate this book to him and his late brother, Mickey, two of the greatest GAA historians in the county.

My mother-in-law, Bridie has always taken a great interest in my writing and has been a huge support in everything I have achieved. The number of cuttings she pulled out of newspapers, of anything her family was involved in, could stretch for miles. The Kennedy home has always been buzzing with GAA chat and it's all been passed on to the next generation. Hopefully, they'll see Derry hands on Sam in Croke Park soon.

From a professional perspective, I'd like to thank the Mallon family, who gave me the opportunity to write for the first time in the *Mid Ulster Observer*. It was the natural progression following my time as PRO of Slaughtneil for more years than I can remember.

I am also proud to have been Sports Editor of the *County Derry Post*, with Derry GAA at the heart of its coverage. A special thanks to all the staff I worked with. I now work for *Gaelic Life*, a dedicated online GAA title and thanks to all my colleagues there for their support every week.

Thanks to all those I have shared a press box with over the years. While it's a pleasure to write about sport, it's a tough and competitive gig and we often lean on each other from time to time.

I would like to thank Liam for providing me the opportunity to write about some of Derry's greatest players and games that chart the history of the Oak Leaf County. His Meath team may have left me in tears on my first trip to Croke Park for the 1987 All-Ireland semi-final, but the fact he trusted me with this piece of work is something I am very proud of. He gave me advice when I needed a steer, and gave me the space when I just needed to get on with it. The monthly contact turned into weekly chats as we got closer to publication. His calm voice always made me feel at ease.

Finally, a huge note of thanks to the 25 Derry stars in this book. I'd often hear school principals say the school is not the building, but rather the staff and students within. This is the same. These men are the book. I am the lucky one who had the chance to help them tell their story. It was an absolute privilege to help chart a day or time in their career they will never forget.

There wasn't a single interview that didn't reveal a nugget, or something I previously didn't know or fully fathom. It was difficult to narrow the players down to the list in this book, given the number of legends who have donned the Oak Leaf over the years. Those chosen, however, brilliantly chart the gaelic football legacy of our county.

It's 30 years since we won our first and only All-Ireland senior title and it's fitting that four of the games from that campaign are recalled in this book. With the current Derry team knocking on the door for Sam, I can only hope that some of the tales in this book can inspire them to take another step closer.

Finally, I never had the pleasure of chatting with Eamonn Coleman. He deserved to have a chapter in this book and I've often wondered which game he'd have picked.

Henry Downey called him 'Mr Derry football himself' minutes after lifting Sam. Thankfully, his memory is threaded through many chapters in this book, as both a player, and an inspirational manager.

Michael McMullan
September 2023

★ INTRODUCTION ★

By Michael McMullan

AS A DERRY fan, writing this book was such an honour. It's especially poignant 30 years after the first and only visit of Sam Maguire to the Oak Leaf County.

The current team has morphed out of an underage production line built to last and back-to-back Ulster senior titles have allowed us to dream big again.

Working on this book over the last year has been an adventure, digging into some of our former greats' most iconic games. I can still picture the evening I went to interview Tony Scullion.

Sitting in his living room, we are sipping tea as Tony's eyes dance with gusto as he recalls the 1990 International Rules series. Words don't do him justice. I glance up at the four All Star awards perched on top of a cabinet. Four! It's the penny dropping moment when you realise you are in the presence of one of the game's finest ever defenders.

Picking 25 players for this book was a tough assignment in itself. Perhaps the toughest.

Getting them to decide on their game was another crossroads. Some knew right away the day their career changed, or the *moment* they'll never forget. For others, it was a wrestle with their memory bank until they made their choice.

Then came the easy bit… shooting the breeze about football, and it has been 12 months of chatting, recording, fact checking and writing.

But my love of Derry goes back further. Back 35 years, all the way to Sunday, March 8, 1987 – the day I attended my first ever Derry game. My godfather, Raymond Scullin was Greenlough chairman at the time and the club were hosting Longford for Derry's penultimate Division Two outing.

He took me along and those memories are there forever. We were among the first to arrive, well before the teams. I recall getting my first programme. It's dog-eared, but I still have it. The jersey numbers of opponents handwritten beside the printed Derry players' names must have denoted the marking arrangements before match-ups were even a thing. An early sign I'd fall into a career of writing about sport.

I can still see the snooker table surface on the Greenlough pitch. The smell of deep heat stands out, and how much curl Enda Gormley could get on the ball. On a day when seven of the players featured in this book were in action, six Gormley points pulled Derry clear, 0-10 to 0-7, and into the top flight as they began their quest towards Sam Maguire six years later.

This came five months after my first ever GAA memory – the 1986 All-Ireland final. Sitting around granny Scullin's TV, we watched on as Tyrone had Kerry on the ropes, before Pat Spillane's acrobatic fisted goal pulled the Kingdom back on their way to glory.

DERRY GREAT, SEAMUS Lagan was my teacher in Glen PS around that time. There was an O'Neill's ball at the front of his classroom. It was an era of one ball between the entire school. We'd take it out every lunch and dinner time for our own All-Ireland finals.

At the time, Slaughtneil's main pitch was being renovated and our early underage training was at the nearby O'Loughlin's field. Trophies and wins were scarce, but I can still see John Joe Kearney taking the time to demonstrate the art of kicking off the ground. He kicked up a tuft of grass and we'd line up to take turns. We placed the ball on it, always with the valve facing up. We'd take a few steps back, run in, lean back… and follow through. Some went over, some didn't.

On a Saturday, Philip McKeown would have us packed into the back of his maroon Austin Allegro on the way to a game somewhere. We lost more than we won, but it didn't quash a love of football that remains as strong as ever. From then, it was on to St Patrick's Maghera where the MacRory Cup visited in five of the seven years I was there. It was an era of Coalisland on St Patrick's Day, of chanting, air horns and flags.

I can still see my name on the noticeboard when the 1995 panel list went up. Magic. I was the sub 'keeper on a team that wrestled past Abbey CBS and St Patrick's Tuam, while hammering everyone else in sight on the way to the Hogan Cup.

Having Adrian McGuckin as a manager is something you never forget. His persistence with the basic skills, his attention to detail and making you feel 10-foot tall were all key ingredients. A coach, manager, tactician and sport psychologist all rolled into one.

When Henry Downey carried Sam into the school sports hall two years earlier, he was followed by half the Derry panel who were past pupils.

The GAA theme continued in my days studying in UUJ, where I had the privilege of serving as chairman of the club in 1997, when I made many connections and lifelong friends from across Ulster. The nights training or chatting over a pint are fond memories.

I had a spell involved in coaching at club and school level in addition to my time with Derry minors. We got to an All-Ireland final and a semi-final during that time. I enjoyed preparing for those days immensely and mixed it with the video analysis side of the game. Being in and around the team environment and seeing players overcome challenges is a special place. It keeps your love of sport alive.

I think that's what makes writing about sport rewarding. Players and coaches pour themselves into the pursuit of their dreams and it's up to us, as writers, to paint the brilliant and varied pictures of emotion. And we must do it with respect. That's our responsibility, but it's a two-way street. For the GAA fraternity, a comfortable level of media engagement is vital for selling the game to those who want to embrace it.

There are so many interesting and excellent stories to be told. That's what I loved about putting this book together. It helped bring back some of my memories of going to watch Derry and I hope you, the reader, have a similar experience.

There wasn't one interview where I didn't pick up something new, or a different context to some of the greatest moments from Derry's history.

Enda Gormley never thought he'd play for Derry and felt that winning Ulster would always be Derry's ceiling. That's what made the All-Ireland final of 1993 the game of his life.

Laurence Diamond's eyes welled up as he recalled the moment when the

Gaels of Bellaghy had a secret homecoming planned after their visit to Croke Park to mark 50 years of winning the All-Ireland Club Championship.

Gary Coleman explained why, as the manager's son, he needed to deliver in the 1992 National League final and convince fans he deserved a starting spot on his own merits.

Enda Muldoon, one of the great ballers, was unsure he had what it took to be a county minor. The summer of '95 answered his questions.

Damian Cassidy explains how beating Down in a Casement classic in '92 was so, so important. There are only so many times you can go to the well. It's a chapter the current Derry squad should digest as they take their steps into 2024.

Kevin McGuckin tells the tale of a depressing bus journey home from Celtic Park with Ballinderry and an entire group of footballers questioning themselves. *Were they finished?* Not by a long shot. Twelve months later, he had the John McLaughlin Cup over his head.

Damian Barton looked out through the raindrops beating against the bus window in Clones in the summer of '93. The weather was irrelevant. They were coming home with the Anglo Celt Cup.

Jim McKeever passed away earlier this year. A giant in Derry as a player, manager and chairman. As well as being one of the all-time greats, being known as 'Gentleman Jim' is quite the legacy. When Derry GAA produced their Centenary Book in 1984, to mark 100 years of the GAA, an excellent photo of McKeever rising like a salmon to make a catch in the 1958 All-Ireland final was prominent. I've often looked at that photo when leafing through the book for some additional facts from Derry's history.

Thanks to the 25 people in this book, the Derry story continues. I hope you enjoy stepping back in time, as much as I did over the last 12 months.

GERRY O'LOUGHLIN

DERRY 3-8 ★ ANTRIM 1-7
Dr McKenna Cup Semi-Final
Dean McGlinchey Park, Ballinascreen
MAY 3, 1970

★ **DERRY:** S Hasson; M McGuckin, H Diamond, T Quinn; P Stevenson, M McAfee, **G O'Loughlin**; T McGuinness, S Lagan; S O'Connell (O-3), M Niblock (O-1), E Coleman (1-2); A McGuckin (2-O), H Niblock (O-1), B Ward. **Sub:** S Gribbin (O-1) for McGuinness.

★ **ANTRIM:** R McIlroy; E Grieve, J Burns, S Killough; B Millar, D Crummey, A Scullion; T McAtamney, F Fitzsimmons; G McCann (O-2), T Dunlop (1-O), L Boyle (O-1); A McCallin (O-4), O Ruddy, R Griffin. **Sub:** D McNeill for Millar.

66

IT IS FAIR to say that I came late to gaelic football and, despite this, I can honestly say that the game has given me lasting memories.

When I look at football today, and the effort put into training kids from as young as four, I am in awe of the journey we have taken. Back in the 60s there was no access to gaelic football until you reached schoolboy-age, which believe it or not was the age of 15.

Some might say that is late to come to the game, but there is no doubt Derry has produced some of the best club and county players in that era.

At the age of 15, I was attending the Tech in Magherafelt, so this was the only opportunity for a young boy who was not attending grammar school. I found myself playing in the forwards and I remained there for club and county.

Those who were attending grammar schools tended to board at either St

THE ACTION

★★★★★

HOLDERS DERRY BOOKED their place in the Dr McKenna Cup final thanks to goals from Adrian McGuckin (two) and Eamonn Coleman.

It was far from a polished performance after bouncing back from a league semi-final defeat at the hands of Mayo. The Saffrons lost midfielder Frank Fitzsimmons early in the second-half, but Derry had the job done by half-time on home soil.

Gerry O'Loughlin was a late inclusion in the side and fitted liked a glove at left half-back in a defence where Henry Diamond and Peter Stevenson both excelled.

It was a tightly congested opening spell that saw the sides level four times by the interval. Proceedings changed after 28 minutes when Eamonn Coleman finished with a gem of a goal, after Adrian McGuckin's involvement earlier in the passage of play. McGuckin also bagged two goals.

Seamus Lagan was impressive at midfield for Derry and while Sean O'Connell showed well in patches, Derry were wasteful in front of the posts.

★★★★★

Columb's in Derry or St Pat's in Armagh. During their absence, this gave players like myself the opportunity to play at county level. They were playing organised football from the age of 11 or 12, which the rest of us never had the opportunity to do.

In 1965, at the age of 18, I was lucky enough to be called into the Derry minor panel and I played a couple of games before the St Columb's or St Pat's students returned to county football. It might seem harsh nowadays. I was so easily replaced by these boys, but I was grateful to have had the opportunity to play at county level and to be on the panel.

I remained as a sub on the minor team for the successful Ulster Championship that year and the All-Ireland series. I was happy to be involved and there is no doubt there were some good players who had attended St Columb's College.

In 1966, I was overage for the minor panel, but I continued to play for the Magherafelt senior team through to the following year. I continued to challenge myself and improve on my game.

We had won a Junior Championship with Magherafelt in 1962 and I played in the forwards. Then, in 1966 and 1967, I asked if I could play right half-back for Magherafelt and this proved to be a good move. I came into my game at this point and continued to play this position.

In 1967, Magherafelt got to the county final, but this was a personally challenging time for me as two weeks prior to this final, when we played Slaughtneil in the semi-final, my father, Patrick died suddenly the young age of 57.

My father was football mad, but unfortunately, he never got the opportunity to see me playing for the county at senior level and this is my one regret. However, he was there when we won the minor All-Ireland, and he was happy I was on the panel and part of it all.

In many ways, football helped me through this time. I found myself focusing on my game. Newbridge beat us by a point in the senior final. There was no shame in that, as they were considered one of the strong teams, alongside Bellaghy and it would have been difficult to say which of the two teams were the best in the county at that stage.

When Down won the All-Ireland in 1968, they beat Derry in the first round, in the 'Battle of Ballinascreen', when I was a sub on the Derry senior team before being picked for the under-21s at left half-back. Things were looking good; we went on to win the Ulster Championship, and beat Offaly in the All-Ireland final.

I played every game through that campaign and when the management made a few changes to give boys a run out at Croke Park in the final, I was one of the those substituted. I was a bit disappointed, but in hindsight it was great to get the opportunity to play at Croke Park. This is the pinnacle of any Gael's football ambition and I was extremely lucky to count myself among the players to achieve this at a young age.

Once again, I was called to the senior team for the Lagan Cup. It was the last year of it and I played a couple of games towards the end of 1967, but it didn't work out for me at all. After that, I only had county football with the juniors in 1969.

IN 1970, I was not involved in the Derry National League panel. Derry got to the semi-final against Mayo, and I remember listening to it on the radio. Mayo were a point in front when Derry had a late free. It needed to go over with the last kick… but it dropped short and the game was over. Derry were out.

Once the dust settled, they had to draw up an Ulster Championship panel and I was delighted to be included for consideration; this meant that if any medals were going later that year, then you were entitled to one. Derry had not won an Ulster Senior Championship since 1958 and they would not have been considered favourites to win, so to even have the opportunity to get a medal was a great honour.

I was called into that panel, and my first game was against Antrim at Ballinascreen in the Dr McKenna Cup. In those days, it was a competition played as a filler before the championship and were deemed as good games to help teams prepare for the upcoming championship.

That call onto the panel was out of the blue. I saw my name in the paper, and I was not expecting it. The team was listed… and my name was among the subs. When I arrived for the game and walked into the dressing-room, Jim McKeever came over.

'You're in!' he told me.

And that was it… I was in at left half-back.

It did not faze me, and I don't know why, maybe I had grown up a bit. I was not a nervous player and even in all the big games Derry played in my time, nerves didn't affect me, and this was no different. I think it was maybe just my nature.

I was used to playing at right half-back, but I had adapted well to playing on the left from my time with the under-21s. I had proven myself to be an adaptable player in any of these positions. Either way, I was happy to play regardless of the position I was playing, and it worked out well for me during this campaign. Looking back, from minor and into under-21, my game had started to toughen up and I had got used to the physical nature of the game.

Football is ingrained in you, and it was part of your everyday life. During this time, I worked in a joinery workshop in Newbridge, and the boss was playing senior football for Newbridge at the time.

There was a small grass area and at lunchtime every day, after our tea, he got us all out to play football. It was not a big area and there was maybe six or seven-a-side, and there were no niceties about it. There was a dashed wall on one side and a thorn hedge on the other side. In the first few months, I couldn't hack it.

It was very physical, and this physicality was a new experience for me, but then eventually you were watching boys throwing their weight about and then something just clicked. It was a case of either forgetting about it, and sitting on your own after the tea, or going out and putting yourself about. I chose the latter and that went on every day for about three years.

I can honestly say that tightened me up. It is wonderful the way things work, and that conditioning carried into the under-21s, and into senior football with Magherafelt, and on with the county.

Back in the workshop, most of the boys were not footballers at all, it was just a kicking session, but it was tough stuff. When you were coming up against that dashed wall you had to have your peripheral vision. If anyone was coming, you needed to be prepared for a hit… either that, or you were going to land in the hedge or up against the sharp dash on the wall.

No doubt you needed your wits about you and this need to focus during these kickabouts helped me to strengthen my own game, as well as teaching me many lessons, including the need to keep my wits about me.

That was around the time I was coming into the Magherafelt senior team, and I had a gained a permanent position within the team, and we were getting ready for the final in 1967.

Looking back on that call to the Derry senior panel for the game against

Antrim in the McKenna Cup, it all came to fruition for me. That was where things started to take off and I played every game from then until I finished with Derry in 1982.

In the last three years, Magherafelt started to play me at left full-back because of my experience and I was good at covering for other players. When you were moved back, you knew you were at the end of your time, but I was still holding a place.

WINNING THE ULSTER Championship in 1970 with Derry was unbelievable. It was the first ever 70-minute Ulster final.

The journey was magnificent, from listening to the All-Ireland final on the radio in 1958 to now... and the realisation this was Derry's first Ulster Championship in 12 years. We were part of it, we were going to play in an All-Ireland semi-final.

Things did not go well for us. We played Kerry and they destroyed us, but it was some thrill to know you had an Ulster Championship medal.

After winning the minor in 1965 and the under-21s three years later, we thought we'd be ready to win the Ulster senior in 1971, but we won earlier than we thought. After winning it and being Ulster champions, we were going for back-to-back the following year, but we went on to play Down in that '71 Ulster final. It was a fantastic game, but we lost 4-15 to 4-11. With Colm McAlarney, Dan McCartan, Sean O'Neill, Down had a good team at that time.

We played them at Casement Park; it was the last Ulster final played there and we just weren't ready for that game. We reckoned it was our year to win Ulster and go onto the All-Ireland. If we had beaten Down, I think we would have beaten Roscommon in the All-Ireland semi-final.

In 1970, I was playing in the GAA Grounds Tournament in London between the winners of all four provinces. It took place after the All-Ireland, with both semi-finals at Wembley. It was a brilliant experience to get playing at Wembley, but the pitch was too small. We were used to playing on bigger GAA pitches at home compared to the smaller soccer pitch... it was very, very tight.

We played Meath who were the Leinster champions at the time, and Kerry beat Galway. Then we played Kerry on the Sunday out in New Eltham where the London GAA grounds were. I do not know how strong a team Kerry had out, but we won it.

It was a brilliant trip, and my first time on a plane. I recall going into the dressing-rooms… the same one as the England team had used in the World Cup. We went in, and there were showers and a big sunken bath. We had never experienced facilities like this before and, as you can imagine, the craic was mighty.

WE WON ULSTER again in 1975 and '76, but the All-Ireland was going to be difficult because Dublin were coming back on the scene again. Them and Kerry were battling it out, they were the two big teams – we met them in the semi-finals both years.

Derry had never met a Connacht team in an All-Ireland semi-final. It was Kerry in 1958, in 1970… and then it was Dublin and Kerry. If we had beaten Armagh in 1977, it would've been Roscommon again.

In 1976, we lost to Dublin in the National League final after we had beaten Cork in the semi-final, but the Dubs beat us in the final, 2-10 to 0-15. Armagh played Dublin in the final of 1977 and if we had beaten Armagh in the Ulster final, we would have been ready for the Dubs and we would've been in a better mental place in the final after being so close in the league, but it wasn't to be.

From 1970 to '82, I started all bar one game, when I came on as sub against Armagh. My last Derry game was up in Irvinestown against Fermanagh, who beat us by a point and went on to the Ulster final. I was 35 at the time and I decided it was time to go, but I had a great career.

I GOT ON the Derry team in 1970 and the following January I was selected to play for Ulster in the Railway Cup. I played in it for four years… we won it in the first year, 1971, when we beat Connacht in the final. Back then, Ulster was always strong.

In that time, I had five All Star nominations but never made the list until 1974 when I was called in as a replacement All Star. Paddy Mullan the county secretary rang me, and I got a letter from Mick Dunne in RTÉ, who was the chairman of the selection committee.

I had to turn it down. Angela and I were married two years and our first child, Garry, was due on the same date as the All Star trip. There was no way I could go. I did not dwell on it. I was happy enough that for the four or five of the years I played for Derry and for Ulster that somebody must have appreciated how well I was doing to have been recognised.

I enjoyed every minute of it. While not winning a senior All-Ireland was a disappointment, I am sure there are plenty of players disappointed at not getting an All-Ireland medal. That would've finished it off nicely… minor, under-21 and senior. I just loved playing, not just for Derry but I just loved playing football.

I have Sean O'Neill's No 14 jersey from the Ulster final of 1975. Sean came over after the game to congratulate us and I asked him for his jersey. 'You can have it certainly. Gerry!' he told me. That jersey was another great memory.

I kept playing for the club until 1992, and I played for Magherafelt Thirds in 1996 when I was 49; when we won the Thirds' Championship against Ballinderry. It was for boys who hadn't made it at senior level… and that medal was like gold for those boys.

I enjoyed my career, and I didn't realise until I had stopped playing, particularly county football, the sacrifices that had been made by my wife, Angela and the fact that she never complained. When we came home from work on the days I had training, she had to deal with the meals and the children, and the same at the weekend if we had an overnight stay for a National League game down the country.

Looking back over my career, it was a great time.

MICKEY NIBLOCK

DOWN 4-15 ★ DERRY 4-11
Ulster SFC Final
Casement Park, Belfast
JULY 25, 1971

★ **DOWN:** D Kelly; B Sloan, D McCartan, T O'Hare (0-1); R McConville, M Denvir, C Ward; D Connolly, D Gordon (0-1); J Murphy (1-1), C McAlarney (0-2), J Morgan (0-6); M Cunningham (2-0), S O'Neill (0-2), D Davey (1-2). **Sub:** M Cole for Morgan.

★ **DERRY:** S Hasson; M McGuckin, H Diamond, T Quinn; P Stevenson, H Niblock, G O'Loughlin; L Diamond, S Gribbin; S O'Connell (0-5), A McGurk (1-2), J O'Leary; A McGuckin, **M Niblock (2-4)**, E Coleman (1-0). **Subs:** M McAfee for H Niblock. MP Kelly for Quinn, T McGuinness for Gribbin.

66

OUR RIVALRY WITH Down began back in 1965 when we won the minor All-Ireland. Even though we only beat them by a point in the Ulster semi-final, it was a deserving win. I was familiar with a lot of the Down players from those days up through to senior level. In minor, into our under-21 seasons and through our early twenties, we were bitter rivals in Ulster.

My brother, Hugh, was a trainee teacher at Trench House in Belfast at the time and a lot of the Down players were at the college with him. Colm McAlarney was one of the best players I came across from that era. He was a young player with Down and was around my age. There were a lot of familiar faces playing against each other quite regularly. For instance, the year after we won the All-Ireland minor title, we played them again.

THE ACTION

★★★★★

TWO LATE GOALS from Mickey Niblock wasn't enough to keep Derry's hands on the Anglo Celt Cup as Down held on to take the glory in front of 30,000 fans at Casement Park.

It was the champions who notched the first two points of the game before Down – with all six of their forwards on the scoreboard – got a grip on matters, pushing 3-11 to 1-7 ahead by half-time.

Anthony McGurk's goal and a point from Sean O'Connell had Derry a goal to the good by the 12th minute before Sean O'Neill stamped his authority on proceedings. O'Neill made a goal for John Murphy before his defence-splitting pass was finished to the net by Michael Cunningham's fist for Down's second of the day.

Cunningham added another goal, with O'Neill and Colm McAlarney involved in the play, and Down had one hand on the cherished silver by half-time.

Derry needed a lift after the break and it was Mickey Niblock who provided it, a pass for Eamonn Coleman to finish past 'keeper Danny Kelly.

Niblock, Coleman and Adrian McGuckin formed an understanding inside, but it was Down who bagged the next goal. A long pass from Murphy was finished to the net by Donal Davey.

James Morgan added points, and Down were 4-12 to 2-9 ahead before Derry's late rally. It was Niblock who grabbed two goals to finish with an impressive tally, but it wasn't enough to stop the Mourne men lifting the cup.

★★★★★

I was captain of Derry and Colm was captain of Down, when they beat us in the Ulster final in '66. I would've played for Ulster in the Railway Cup at that time as well with a lot of those great Down men. Players like Dan McCartan, James McCartan, Paddy Doherty, Sean O'Neill and Colm were there too.

By the time we reached under-21, we went all the way to the All-Ireland final where we beat Offaly, so our group of Derry players were growing in confidence. I was looking back through the scrapbooks and remember it saying somewhere that I might have just been awarded Man of the Match in that final 'by a whisker'.

I can remember their captain Eugene Mulligan fouling me in the first-half and getting sent off that day. They also had a great side that went on to win a senior All-Ireland… and Offaly, they always had good, tough, players.

The basis of that Derry under-21 team stayed together and were drafted in to play with the seniors, and that's where we'd have played Down again that year in the championship in Ballinascreen; the game they have always talked about as the 'Battle of Ballinascreen'.

Ray McConville, he was sent out to man mark me that day. As with the other markers over the years, like Patsy Forbes from Tyrone, they were just man-markers. They'd just stick to you like glue. Patsy was man marking me one night and when I came home my mother told me I should've hit him a belt because he was nearly pulling the jersey off me.

A funny story emerged from the next day. Patsy was just getting his furniture business up and running at the time. I came home from my break at work and there was Patsy in my mother's house. She had ordered a suite of furniture and I told her he was the boy that had the jersey off me. She had just bought the furniture off him and couldn't believe it.

Looking back to that day in Ballinascreen, Ray and myself, we got into a bit of a scuffle and both of us got sent off… and that was the main thing I remember about that day. I recall how you can be drawn into this kind of thing and there was no more participation in the game; it was an awful feeling to be sent off.

I HAD MADE my Derry senior debut a few years earlier when I was called in during my time with the minors. From those early days, I fondly remember how much I enjoyed the camaraderie, how much I loved the game and going to training. It was just great being involved in those days.

Jim McKeever was one of the main players in those days and would've been known across Ireland. I was 19 when I was called into play in the Railway Cup. At that time, the great Mick Higgins of Cavan was the manager of the Ulster team. Just to see the tradition, to see these famous names and to be in among them, it was a great feeling and gave you the appetite for more.

As a young player, you can go in with no fear and play with abandonment. It's like a freedom, but you can get a rude awakening too. I remember playing a 'carnival game' in Antrim one night and I went to tackle one of the Hardys from Rasharkin. He flew back his hand and hit me on the side of the head, and I thought I was blinded for life. The games were tough back in those days.

In my playing days, I had a good dummy and a body swerve that took me into space, but the type of player I didn't like playing against were the smaller ones. I came up against some tough players. I would say Tom Prendergast from Kerry would've been one of my most tricky opponents when we played in Croke Park back in those days. He was right half-back and I'd be up against him on the wing.

With my style of play, I'd give the bigger fellas a dummy and they wouldn't come back at you, but Tom was like a little terrier. If you sold him a dummy, he was almost back immediately. You just couldn't shake him off.

John Morley, God rest him, from Mayo was another. He was a detective who got shot in a bank robbery and I would've come up against him in those provincial games against Connacht. He was an excellent player.

You also had John O'Keeffe of Kerry. I played full-forward against him in the 1970 All-Ireland semi-final. When I think back, he always had a little shirt-pull before the ball came in. He was one of the more astute players and he'd often play in front of you. I think a lot of defenders now should take a chance and stand out in front of their opponent. You often see the ball coming in low or chest high, and I can't believe it now when I see how many defenders are caught inside their man.

John stood in front of me and I thought, *Oh my God, I never saw this before…* because I was expecting to run out and get an easy ball. If he wasn't standing in front of me, he gave your jersey a wee tug from behind and stepped out in front of you. There was a steep learning curve against the Kerry boys, but they did it very discreetly, I must say.

We had won Ulster senior in 1970 and it was nice to add to the collection after the earlier minor and under-21 All-Irelands, but our group of players, we were aiming a bit higher than that, but unfortunately, it didn't materialise.

Over the 70s, Derry got to Croke Park for semi-finals, but came up short and my recollection of coming up short in 1970 was that the stamina wasn't there. Looking at the squad, we had as good a bunch of players as anybody in the country at that time and we really should've won an All-Ireland. Basically, if I was asked why we didn't, it was fitness levels. Fellas were coming to training and we didn't know if they had injuries or not.

It told when we got to Croke Park. Kerry beat us in the last 10 minutes or so in a lot of those important games. We drew with them three years later in the league final and we wouldn't play the replay because of an issue with the referee.

I just put it down to a lack of fitness in some of our lads and maybe that came from being out through injury, and not being able to train properly and that went against us in those games. After minor and under-21, it was a big disappointment that we didn't go all the way.

WE WERE BACK in the Ulster final the following year, 1971, and even though we were the champions, we knew what we were up against with Down in the final.

There was no chance of us being in any way complacent because it was always tit for tat when Derry and Down met over those years. This was no different. They were All-Ireland champions three years earlier and the Down reputation always went before them. Even this year, when the current Down team scored eight goals against Laois in the Tailteann Cup, people were saying not every team scores eight goals in Croke Park. Conor Laverty has done what I said we should've done with Derry. They looked like a team who had a good pre-season and a lot of hard work has been put in. Then you can go down to Croke Park and play the football you want to when you are fit.

Down have always had good footballers. In our day, they had a good blend of players. Paddy Doherty, Sean O'Neill, Joe Lennon, James McCartan... and, in defence, they had Tom O'Hare. I played four seasons with Ulster and I had built up a great relationship with most of those Down men. I was just a teenager and recall how well Dan McCartan helped me to settle in, he was very welcoming and made you feel at home. And Sean O'Neill was the same. We seemed to get on well when we met socially, but all that was forgotten out on the pitch. Even with Ray McConville, who had ended my game that day in Ballinascreen.

I played in a lot of excellent games, but I always have a fond memory of how I played in that 1971 Ulster final. There was a huge crowd at Casement that day, but I still thought Clones was a better ground for finals. It seemed like the crowd were right in on top of you, whereas in Casement there was like a dyke the whole way around the pitch. Down got off to a flying start and had a game-winning lead built up by half time. It was a disappointing game for us as a team, but anytime you score 2-4 in a match it is going to be special. I played across the half forward line most of my career. Brendan Devlin would've been in the centre and I would've been on the wing, but in later years it was mainly at centre forward or midfield. It wasn't that often I played at full-forward, but I did that day against Down, and also in Croke Park that day on John O'Keeffe and Padraig Donoghue.

With my father, Hugh being a soccer player, there was an interest in the soccer. It was my uncle Frankie, who won a league medal in '47. It was him and my mother who influenced us to concentrate on the Gaelic, even though I played soccer when I was studying at the Tech. One of my ploys when I was playing at centre half-forward was, I'd run in to try and block the kickout. I made it look like I wanted to block it but knew I wasn't going to get it. It was more about getting the centre half-back to come in with me, to take him out of position… and I would just turn and get a breaking ball from the middle of the field.

It was the same when players were coming down the wing and crossing it into the square. Everyone was going into the square like Brown's cows, and I would hang back off the parallelogram and the melee… and get a breaking ball for an easy point.

Those are the little things I remember. It was reading the game, which came from soccer coaching and watching a bit of soccer. I found those ploys worked for me. Even years later, when I was a selector for Cork and Nicholas Murphy was playing in the middle of the field; I noticed Nicholas going to catch every ball. I waited to half-time and told him he was up against some of the best midfielders in Ireland… 'You won't catch every ball'.

'On their kickout, you go up and punch it forward… then your job is done and it is up to the forwards to get the loose ball.' I see Conor Glass, as a defensive midfielder, punching the ball and I think it deflates your opponent.

Soccer brought that to my game; it was the thinking off the ball, drawing your opponent into a false area on the field and a false sense of security. I inherited it from my father, who was a good soccer player and it was something I was blessed with. When I went to New York, I played some of my best football out there in Gaelic Park, but the standard wasn't the same as it was back home. The thing about my game was that I had good vision, it was one of my attributes.

When I think back to our Derry team, I wouldn't have been a speedster like Eamonn Coleman, but I had good vision and could see the tackles coming; thankfully, I avoided a lot of them. The full-forward line that day in Casement Park…it was myself, Eamonn and Adrian McGuckin. The three of us crossed paths as schoolboys. All the way up, we played together for Derry minors, the under-21s and into the seniors. I think Eamonn made his senior debut for Ballymaguigan when he was a schoolboy and we nicknamed him James McCartan, because he just was a flying machine.

Eamonn, Adrian and I would've hit it off well and it helped in that 1971 Ulster final. I scored two goals and set up one for Eamonn. With Eamonn, he knew that if I was going up to field a ball, I was always able to flick it on and he'd be onto it like a hare. He got a lot of scores from going through like that. With his low centre of gravity he'd be hard to catch.

By the time Derry won Ulster again in 1975 and '76, I was in New York. I had been going over and back for games from '69 to '71, before settling there in 1972. When I came back to Ireland, I played for Douglas where I won an intermediate title and also travelled up to win the 1978 Derry championship with Magherafelt, before moving to play for Nemo Rangers.

I played under Billy Morgan and Jim Cremin. When you look at the forwards back defending now, Billy had them pressing even back then. Their motto was hunt in packs, like Barcelona. With Barcelona, if you lose possession, you've to get it back very quick and that's what Billy and Jim did with Nemo. You need to instil that in players. The buzz word for me is fitness and these modern players are so fit.

LAURENCE DIAMOND

BELLAGHY 0-15 ★ UCC 1-11
All-Ireland Club SFC Final
Croke Park, Dublin
MAY 12, 1972

★ **BELLAGHY:** P McTaggart; T Scullion, A Mulholland, F Cassidy; T Diamond (0-1), H McGoldrick, C Brown; **L Diamond**, P Doherty (0-1); F Downey (0-1), B Cassidy (0-3), F O'Loane (0-7); H Donnelly, T Quinn (0-2), K Cassidy.

★ **UCC:** N Murphy; J Gleeson, M Keane, J Coughlan; J O'Grady, S Looney, T Looney; P Lynch (0-2), N O'Sullivan (0-1); B Lynch (0-2), R Bambury, D Murray; D Coffey (0-5), D Kavanagh (1-1), N Brosnan. **Sub:** S Murphy for Brosnan.

66

GROWING UP AROUND Bellaghy, we had no other distractions only football and going to different fields to play. At that time, the club didn't have a permanent home. We were playing on pitches like Heaney's field and McCloy's field, different places around the parish.

I can vividly remember the first changing room we had at McCloy's field. It was a railway carriage. Before that, you stripped off and your clothes were put on a hedge down in the corner of a field.

We had big six-inch nails hammered into the railway carriage and thought it was great that we could hang up our clothes and they'd be dry. Those memories are still very clear. My first championship was in 1963, coming on as a sub against Newbridge.

THE ACTION

★★★★★

A LATE BRENDAN Cassidy point clinched All-Ireland glory for Bellaghy after an enthralling contest that saw the sides level on five occasions in a gripping second-half.

A UCC side, powered by Kerry duo Paudie and Brendan Lynch, also had Moss Keane in their ranks at full-back. With three minutes to go, Brendan Lynch kicked the students into the lead for just the second time in the game... only for the Tones to finish with a flourish.

The only disappointment came with the realisation that 1971 champions, East Kerry, failed to return the trophy and Bellaghy left Croke Park empty-handed.

The Ulster champions had the aid of the breeze in the first-half and led 0-8 to 0-5 with Frankie O'Loane displaying an array of attacking prowess. UCC were on level terms midway through the second-half, when Brendan Lynch's free from the wing was punched to the net by Donal Kavanagh.

Bellaghy pulled ahead, but back came UCC to go ahead late on. It was time to regroup and a swift Bellaghy counter-attack saw Tom Quinn fouled, and O'Loane levelled matters again.

This time, the Tones would not be denied. A UCC attack was repelled by Hugh McGoldrick and the blues went on the attack, with Brendan Cassidy kicking the winning score.

★★★★★

In the early Bellaghy teams, as schoolboys, we used to walk or go on bicycles out to play football and the field would be packed every night at that time. There were men standing across the endline, in the goals… and there was the same about 50 yards out. The ball would be flying in an out and they'd be battling away to get their hands on it. That was how the football practice looked back then; there was no real structure to it in any shape or form.

As schoolboys, football in Derry was organised across the three boards… North Derry, South Derry and the City, so you'd play with the teams in your area. On top of those games, there were the carnivals arranged around the clubs and you'd often go there as a schoolboy to play. The winners might end up getting 10 shillings in prize money. You'd head away on bicycles, sometimes down to Clady and different places. There would be two or three games, and you'd head back home with the boots tied on the bar of the bike.

Those were the early memories of playing on the teams as we grew up, but football was central to everything. Nearly every night we'd be going out to watch the seniors play. Then, during the summer holidays, you'd be out there playing every day.

The senior teams before that era had players like Gerry McCann and Dan Joe Cassidy, and I can recall playing with both of them when I started. They had won championships before that, all the way back to when Bellaghy won their first title in 1956. After that, there were championships coming fairly regularly to the club.

THE YEAR BEFORE our All-Ireland campaign, we lost the 1970 county final to Newbridge. Back then, ourselves and the 'Bridge were always a chart-topper. We were the top teams at that time and we'd have knocked lumps out of each other on the pitch and then carried each other off the field.

There was no animosity. The two clubs backed each other back them. There was a respect and a great camaraderie between the teams, but in the games themselves there was blood and thunder. Those were good days.

We came back the following year to win the championship and we beat Lavey in the final. Then, the year after we won the All-Ireland, we lost to Ballinascreen in the county final. It was disappointing, but you accepted that… the wins and defeats. The bunch of boys we had in Bellaghy at that time; we were together for a number of years. There was a core in the team. With that togetherness, you knew each other's style and the type of football they played.

It was probably one of the first outfits in Bellaghy that played football. We just didn't put our heads down and kick the ball into the air and catch it again. It was the start of the evolution. It probably began to change in around 1968, the late 60s. We won the Ulster Club Championship for the first time that year, in the first year of the competition, beating St Joseph's Ballyshannon in the final. They had Brian McEniff on board; they were some outfit.

I am not too sure what exactly changed with the style of our play, it seemed to just evolve. It possibly came through the schools who were bringing in a coaching strategy that transferred to the clubs. St Columb's won a Hogan Cup in 1965. Maybe from that, we tapped into those lines as well but the coaching did get a bit more structured.

We had a trainer and manager around that time. There was nothing else involved, not like the management teams we have now. If you were lucky enough, you had a doctor at the match. We had Dr Hugh Glancy, who was a former chairman of the club, so he was always available to look after us. Harry Cassidy was the manager and Tommy Gribbin came in as the trainer for the 1972 All-Ireland semi-final and final.

THE TEAM WE had; we were very much a tight unit. There were no prima-donnas and we all worked and played for each other.

That was something that came from our youth. We had won schoolboy and minor titles along the way, so that success all helped as we moved up into the senior team. We had a bond between us from a very early age, right up to the end. I finished playing for Bellaghy in 1979 when we were beat by Scotstown in the Ulster Championship.

Another thing that helped us was that we didn't lose any players. You hear nowadays of people going to America and Australia, but with our team, we held on to everybody. With the success we were having in Derry, there were thoughts towards going a bit further. You always knew, and it was a well-known fact back then, that the Derry championship was always going to be the hardest one to win, no matter who you were playing.

If you won that, then when the Ulster Championship started you had a big chance of competing against anybody. That year in Ulster, we played Letterkenny and beat them after a replay in Magherafelt. We also played Ardboe and Teemore, before meeting Clan na nGael of Armagh in the final. They were favourites, but we didn't see it that way. We were racking up the scores in the previous two matches and we knew we had the firepower up front to do the damage no matter who we were playing.

The thing about winning the Derry Championship, once you win a match in Ulster, your confidence is sky high anyway and you think you can go on and win it. I remember that day against Clan na nGael, it was a shocking poor day and it was the same in 1968 when we played Ballyshannon. We got off to a great start and were 1-9 to 0-2 up in the rain. At the time, the weather was seen as helping us, but we were equally happy playing on dry days as well.

There was a great feeling to have won it again. Ulster was the pinnacle in 1968 with the All-Ireland campaign not starting until 1971. This time we had another focus and our minds began to look ahead to the All-Ireland, and our game against Portlaoise in the semi-final.

We played them in Magherafelt and they could've beaten us that day. The teams were level five times. It took Hughie Donnelly's point in the last minute. That's how tight that game was. We were behind and after Frankie O'Loane equalised, Hugh's score won it. Before that, our toughest game in Ulster was against Letterkenny when we needed a replay.

When I think back to the excitement of preparing for the All-Ireland… I remember our main pitch being developed at that time, out the Ballyscullion Road. We were training on the bottom of the pitch, the flat part… and Austin Mulholland, the full-back on our team, put up a few lights and poles so we could train. Then, when we were finished, we were mucked to the eyeballs and we went down into the mill river beside the pitch to wash our legs… so that was our ice bath. Those were great times; it was a wonderful time to be living through.

We had that feeling that we could win an All-Ireland and there was the excitement of having everybody in the parish behind you. We had all the help we needed and the support we got was very important. The build-up was great and I remember us leaving on the bus from the Diamond in Bellaghy on the day of the game and all the spectators waving us away. We were heading off to Dublin and the big unknown in Croke Park.

We didn't know much about UCC at the time. We knew they were a formidable outfit with Cork and Kerry players, and with other players from across Munster on the team. There was talk about their jersey at the time and we knew it was a bit different with the skull and crossbones on it. I suppose it could've been a bit intimidatory if you saw it for the first time, wondering what it was… so we sent to Croke Park for a jersey.

We got one and we put it on some unsuspecting player at training and worked around him to make sure the jersey wasn't going to intimidate us.

When we got to Croke Park, we were in the old changing rooms under the Cusack Stand. In that game, the memories went in a flash from the throw-in, until the last kick of the ball. One memory was Tom Quinn's tussle with Mossie Keane that day, with Mossie going on to be an international rugby player. One could say that it was Tom's speed that won out against Mossie's enthusiasm.

The game itself was a ding-dong battle all the way through; they were Sigerson Cup winners that year, so they were coming off a winning streak. They got a goal and it took us a while to peg it back, right until Brendan Cassidy kicked the winner.

UCC went a point up, but we got the last two scores and I remember Brendan's shot going over for a point off the post. We had to hold out with about five minutes to go. Afterwards, there was no presentation because East Kerry didn't give back the trophy from the previous year. But at the final whistle there was utter pandemonium as our loyal supporters invaded Croke Park and surrounded the team in unbridled scenes of joy.

When we eventually got back into the changing room, it was then that the enormity of the event sank home and there was an explosion of pure euphoria. Tears were streaming down grown men's faces and many from founder members of the club who had lived to see the pinnacle reached.

East Kerry were a divisional team, made up of six clubs, so you could say that Bellaghy was the first 'single club' to have won the All-Ireland club title. We had a great team. In defence, we had Tom Scullion and my brother, Tommy. Hughie McGoldrick was centre-half and his younger brother, John was the youngest on the panel. I think he was 16 at that time. Austin Mulholland was full-back and Paddy McTaggart was the goalkeeper, but in those days, it was always the full-back who kicked the ball out. Chris Brown and Frankie Cassidy were also in the defence and they were two tenacious tacklers. We had the measure of them in our defence even though they had a classy forward line.

At midfield there was myself and Francis Downey. Peter Doherty would've been my usual midfield partner, but he was a third midfielder at that stage, before they had ever really been invented. Brendan Cassidy was centre half-forward; Tom Quinn was up at full forward with Kevin Cassidy and Hughie Donnelly. Frankie O'Loane was in the attack too and was a great scorer for us. On the panel we also had Sean Lee, Bobby Milne, Sean O'Neill, John McGoldrick, Colm Hickson, Sean Hickson, Ben McCann and Liam Horley. Sean Lee and Bobby Milne in particular had made serious contributions to our Derry and All-Ireland campaigns.

To quote from Willie Cassidy's book, *Gaelic in Blue and White*, published in 1969, he said, 'Soon the club will be 30 years old, let us hope by then, it will have an addition to its Derry and Ulster crowns – the title All-Ireland champions'.

Willie had to wait only three more years, and that was achieved and he was there to see it.

WINNING AN ALL-IRELAND tops it all and it was a brilliant night. We came home to Bellaghy and were taken up through the town in Harry Cassidy's fruit and vegetable lorry. I remember us all standing on the back of it. There were crowds of people there to see us home… it doesn't get any better than that. Even 50 years later, people still look to that team and have a great respect for the men who played on it.

Bryansford beat us in an Ulster semi-final the year before when they went to the All-Ireland final and those boys still have an affiliation for our club here in Bellaghy. We still meet up with them regularly and the clubs still have a relationship.

We had our 50th reunion of the All-Ireland last year and it was another night to remember. The crowds that were there that night were unbelievable. The club took us all to Dublin for the day. The Kilcoo boys came to the Carrickdale that morning with the cup. We took it to Dublin and got it presented to us by the GAA President in the Hogan Stand.

Thomas Niblock came with us to record it all, from the moment we left home, to the food in the Carrickdale… to being in and around Croke Park. We came home to Bellaghy that night, up over McKeefry's brae and coming towards Bellaghy Bawn on our way from Toome… I remember sitting beside Frankie

Cassidy on the bus and he said, 'There must be a serious match on in Bellaghy tonight'. All we could see was traffic.

We arrived on the bus and the club car park was lined from the road right up to the hall with all the young teams from the club. It was a fabulous sight, something I will never forget. They were waiting on the team coming home. It was 50 years later but it was lovely to see.

The place was packed and that tells you what it still means to the people of Bellaghy... and a lot of them weren't even there back in the 70s, but they wanted to be there to see us coming home. The whole thing was organised by the people on the current club committee. When we were away in Dublin, the homecoming was put together and we knew nothing about it.

The youngsters were there, all in their club gear to see a pile of old boys coming back from Dublin. It was marvellous.

We never got the cup at any point after we won the All-Ireland in 1972. We never as much as laid eyes on it, but we came home with the cup anyway... 50 years later. We carried in into Bellaghy club that night as if we had won it that day.

MICKEY LYNCH
(& GERRY McELHINNEY)

DERRY 1-16 ★ DOWN 2-6
Ulster SFC Final
St Tiernach's Park, Clones
JULY 27, 1975

★ **DERRY:** J Somers; M McAfee, T Quinn, G Bradley; P Stevenson, A McGurk, G O'Loughlin; E Laverty (0-1), T McGuinness (0-2); **G McElhinney (1-1), M Lynch (0-5)**, B Kelly; J O'Leary (0-2), S O'Connell (0-5), M Moran. **Subs:** S Lagan for McAfee, K Teague for Lagan.

★ **DOWN:** L McAlinden; B Sloan, D McCartan, P Galbraith; P Hamill, C Digney, M Slevin; C McAlarney, D Connelly; J Murphy (0-1), P Rooney (0-2), D Morgan; M Cunningham, S O'Neill, W Walsh (2-3). **Subs:** M Turley for Slevin, D Gordon for Connelly, B Fitzsimons for Digney.

66

MY FIRST TIME in with Derry was with the minors in 1970 when we won Ulster with Martin O'Neill on the team. I was only 15 at the time, but I was on the training panel.

We played the All-Ireland semi-final against Kerry before the senior's semi-final with Kerry. The hurlers were down too, so it was three Derry teams all playing in Croke Park on the same day... and all lost.

I was not supposed to be togging out in the match day panel, but they were short players, so I got the call to take my gear. So, I was togged out that day even though I was never going to get on the team. That was the first time I was involved with Derry.

THE ACTION

★★★★★

AN EARLY GOAL from Gerry McElhinney set the tone for an emphatic Derry victory as they got their hands on the Anglo Celt Cup for the first time in five seasons.

The Oakleafers played to their full potential with a style of open play that was refreshing on the eye, culminating in 1-12 of their tally coming from open play.

The foundation for victory was the boundless running of McElhinney and Man of the Match Mickey Lynch, who kicked five points from play, that had Down playing second fiddle.

The pivotal moment of the game arrived as early as the third minute. Lynch's high ball towards Sean O'Connell, who was up against Dan McCartan, had Down under pressure. The onrushing McElhinney latched onto the ball to finish to the net.

At the other end of the field, Tom Quinn had a fine game on Down star Sean O'Neill, but Derry needed a portion of fortune. Willie Walsh did manage a Down goal, but they were denied by the woodwork on three further occasions. Walsh hit both post and crossbar, while Dan McCartan's penalty came off the inside of the upright before spinning away to safety.

Derry were 1-8 to 1-5 ahead at the break, and despite a second Walsh goal they kicked on to round off a deserving victory.

★★★★★

We didn't get to any Ulster finals in my three other minor seasons after that, but I was captain of the under-21 team in 1976 when we won Ulster and were beaten by Kildare in the All-Ireland semi-final.

I played my first senior match in the league in October 1974, against Tyrone in Ballinascreen. Phelim Hugh Forbes was marking me that day; I was taken off and I never got back on the team until the following year.

Liam Hinphey was part of the management at that time and he landed at the house one day, saying he knew things didn't go too well but they wanted me and Fintan McCloskey in the panel, and how they were getting Gabriel Bradley and all the young boys back on again before the start of the league for the 1974-75 season.

We were getting some league games here and there, until some of the older players retired. Sean O'Connell, Malachy McAfee, Gerry O'Loughlin and Adrian McGuckin were still about, boys from that age-group. Then you had players like Anthony McGurk and Tom McGuinness on board as well.

The previous season, we didn't do much but it changed for the championship in 1975. After beating Armagh in the first round, we were through to play Monaghan in the semi-final in Dungannon. The first game ended up in a draw and I remember it well. I was picked up by Eamon Tavey. He was a hard-hitting opponent, and we marked each other on many occasions.

Eugene Laverty got a penalty at the very end, with time almost up. Peter Stevenson stepped up to slot home the pressure kick to draw the game. That penalty was our lifeline. It was the last kick of the game and we'd have been out of the championship, that's how close it was.

We went on to beat them in the replay, and Tavey got booked twice and was sent off before the end, but things changed before the second game. Sean O'Connell, to be fair, was the man that changed things at training. Frankie Kearney, Seamus Kelly and Liam Hinphey were there that time as the management team. Sean didn't say a while lot, but everyone listened to him, including the management.

We were training at Ballinascreen the week after the drawn game... and he just sat us down. He spoke about how things didn't totally work 'the last day' and we needed to tweak a few things. Sean was playing at full-forward and urged us in the half-forward line to stay out, and for everyone to kick the ball over us and into himself and whoever was playing in the two corners.

The next part, he told us, were the boys in the half-forward line... we had the young legs to do all the running and we'd run in after the ball to support the men inside. It was a case of having boys who were quick and could move over the ground, so we had to use them.

To be fair to Sean and the way he played, he never turned and took his man on with the ball. He would always win possession and come out until you met him. It was Sean who pulled it all together and he was a great player himself. That's what he was very good at and when he received the ball, opponents couldn't take it off him.

This approach to forward play is what he thought would work, and we all took it on board into the games.

WE PLAYED DOWN in the 1975 Ulster final, but we did quite a good bit of training for the championship earlier that year, or what we thought was a lot of training compared to what the players are doing now.

We'd have trained two days a week, and a Saturday morning; then you went to Timoney's in Ballinascreen for your pint of milk. We'd training sessions in Bellaghy a few times as well in those days... and this was all at the start of the Troubles too.

Many a night, and later on in life, you'd be stopped by the army on our way to or from training. You'd be put out and the bags emptied upside down... and you emptied upside down. You could've been kept for an hour... especially coming from Bellaghy, out that Knockloughrim road.

Then we had a guy Billy Lunn, who started with us as a physio. He travelled to training with us; he was a physio with the army in England. He'd show his badge and once they saw that, we'd be straight through. It made some difference. There would've been me, Fintan McCloskey, Liam Murphy, Peter Stevenson and sometimes Gerry McElhinney, depending on where he was, but that would've been the load. Wee Francie Donaghy would've been driving the car. The schedule is not like it is now.

Back then, there was a gap of eight or ten weeks from the league to the championship. Of that, there would've been three or four weeks of hills and dales up around Ballinascreen. Then, for the last two weeks coming up to the championship, training would've shortened up and we'd have been using the ball. Before that, there would've been six weeks when we never saw a ball.

Our schedule had us training during the week; there'd be a team talk on the Saturday morning, and then you played a game at the weekend.

Also, during that time, Tom McGuinness and myself would've been doing our own extra training at lunchtime. He was involved in building work at the time and I started a job in Derry, and we'd meet up in Celtic Park. It was more or less from the start of the year, and we'd meet up a couple of days during the week with the army standing there looking at us.

McGuinness was always in good shape and we always thought we were quicker than each other, and we had that rivalry. We trained together up and down the pitch, then we'd be back to work… soaked with sweat.

AFTER WE DREW with Monaghan in the championship, we realised we had a good side. Monaghan would've been favourites that day. We drew with them when that penalty got us a replay. In the second game, we played them off the park but they played for 20 or 25 minutes with a man down.

We had Down in the final and I remember the preparation. Down were hot favourites with players such as Sean O'Neill, even though he was coming to the end of his career, and Colm McAlarney. We were coming out of nowhere and we had no chance, that was how it was perceived.

We were in good form though. All the club football was going well at the time. It was different to the present day. We'd have played a lot of football with the club; they didn't miss out. You'd have been playing with the club all the way through the county season.

I saw me leaving an Ulster semi-final to go and play in a 'carnival cup' final that evening. Other times, you left Dublin, from an All-Ireland semi-final and maybe beat off the park, but you came all the way back home and played for your club that night.

There was no such thing as not playing… you played for your club and your county. That was everybody, all over. The only elite ones were Kerry; they were a law onto themselves, and they had the team to be a law onto themselves.

For that final in Clones, I can remember coming out of the changing rooms and you were trembling on the pitch at the start, coming down those steps. I remember Hinphey going about slapping the jaws of everybody before we came down onto the pitch; he could see we were all nervous.

We got a good start that day which was a big help. I think we had 1-1 on the board before they even scored. The team, in general, all played well. We had Tom Quinn at full-back and Tom McGuinness in the middle of the field. Eugene Laverty played in that one as well.

It wasn't as much the early goal; I think it was our performance that sapped them. They had Sean O'Neill on and he never touched the ball. Before the game, it was all about what he'd do with us, but he never got a kick of it. It was the Damper, Peter Stevenson, who marked him, but then he'd put the fear of God in you anyway.

The early goal had the fingerprints of our plan from that training session in Ballinascreen all over it. Gerry McElhinney got it. It was a one-two with me, and then I put it into O'Connell… then McElhinney just came past him, took the ball and stuck it in the net.

Down had a corner-forward that nearly beat us on his own that day, Willie Walsh. We lost Malachy McAfee early on with injury and they put Seamus Lagan back into mark him. Out of Down's 2-6, Willie scored 2-3 of it and he gave us a lot of bother.

The winning of that game was our team performance. Anthony McGurk, Peter Stevenson, Tom Quinn,… we all played really well that day. I can remember that game like I can remember yesterday. I hit five points, and Sean O'Connell hit the same; he'd have been taking the frees and was very accurate. McElhinney got the goal to set us up. Johnny O'Leary, Eugene Laverty and Tom McGuinness all got points too, whereas Down, they had only one real scorer.

I got Man of the Match that day, but I would've been playing good football for the club at the time. I didn't feel any better in Clones that day than any other, you just went out and played. In the games against Monaghan, I was scoring well too.

It's not like now where they don't put the ball into the full-forward. They play a very defensive game. That wasn't our game. The younger legs were told to attack, attack… attack, and if we got the frees, we'd have boys to put the ball over the bar.

Brendan Kelly was wing half-forward, I would've been in the centre and Gerry McElhinney was on the left. Mickey Moran was at corner-forward, you had Sean in the middle and Johnny O'Leary in the other corner.

The change to our approach after the drawn game with Monaghan made the difference. The ball had to be played over ourselves in the half-forward line and into the full-forward line at all times, then we'd come off the shoulder as such.

That's the way it was played. You worked it out from defence and when it got within kicking distance, you had to leave it in. There was no such thing as turning to go back in again like they do today.

Tom McGuinness lorded the middle of the field and he was playing against Colm McAlarney, who I would've classed at that time as the best in Ulster, and I'd say the best player in Ireland was Jack O'Shea.

Eugene Laverty, he got all the breaking ball, he was very underrated. He was a big strong man and he could also use the ball. Winning in Clones sticks out for me because it was our first Ulster Senior Championship medal, and we went on the following year to win another. We could've made it three in-a-row in 1977 against Armagh. I could write a book about it. We were hot, hot favourites and were played off the park.

An Ulster title for a Banagher man was great and we had three men on the panel, it was quite an achievement. We didn't win an All-Ireland, but we thought we had a good side and got to three Ulster finals with that squad. We played none against Dublin. We were whacked that day, stuffed.

You can blame this and you can blame that but things just didn't go our way. The same thing happened in the 1976 league final. The semi-final we played against Kerry in '76, we were up at half-time and they scored five goals in the second-half.

The craic was good in the camp and the panel was very strong. Generally, everybody was at training. The odd fella would've had an excuse here and there, but we all turned up to training whether you liked it or hated it.

Anthony McGurk was maybe the best player Derry had on that team at centre half-back. He always scored a point himself and set up more scores. He would have given and taken a pass in midfield and left it into the forwards.

The fouls were a foul then. It's not like the stuff now. You were half-killed and you knew it was a foul. It was hard football and it was the same in the club games. It was to see who could compete with each other the hardest and still get the ball.

I could've run back then and we would've had the argument with Sean Marty Lockhart here in the club over which of us was the quickest. I was doing the 100 metres in 10 seconds and we didn't have the training he had. During my playing career, I did *Superstars* as well and we'd have tramped the road quite a bit. We did it locally here, the Northern Ireland version of it… down in Bobby Farren's gym.

The first, second and third placed went down south. I went to the All-Ireland one and was beaten into second place. It would start off with a four-mile road run, then you had so many sit-ups and so many pull ups. There was a cycle and swim… but I didn't do that. You were allowed to miss out one event, and I couldn't swim.

You were always keeping yourself fit. I think back to the three years before Derry won the All-Ireland. I was on that panel with Coleman at the very start in 1990, when I was 35.

He had boys running up in the Mary Peters' track two or three nights a week. They were up and down hills, dales and fields… you name it, they were at it. This is what Kerry had done to win Sam, because Eamonn Coleman and Fr Hegarty met Mick O'Dwyer down in Dundalk to get a training regime from him.

He told them if they followed that, in two or three years they'd win the All-Ireland and, to the date, it happened.

★★★★★

GERRY McELHINNEY

"

I REMEMBER WHEN I was playing for Banagher and Seamus Hasson was the county goalkeeper at the time.

Seamus Gormley lived on a farm at the bottom of our lane, it was Seamus who got me involved with Banagher, introducing me to the underage.

Seamus Hasson played on the Derry team that won Ulster in 1970 and I used to tune into their games. You could only hear it on the radio, me and my dad and my mam used to sit down and listen to the action from across the country.

It was different back then, you couldn't see it and had to make up your own mind on how it was going from what you heard. That was the start of the 70s, I was at secondary school then and I was aware of what Derry was all about. I didn't know all the players because, in those days, you couldn't really get to the games as easily as you can now. You had to wait until Banagher were up against the likes of Ballerin, and you'd see Sean O'Connell playing. I never went to a Derry game until I played for Derry against Antrim at Magherafelt… I never saw them play.

It was 1975 and a Dr McKenna Cup when I got a call from Frankie Kearney to be in Magherafelt at 1.30 for a game. I was playing with Celtic at the time and was coming back from Glasgow. My dad picked me up at the airport to take me to the game.

I walked into the dressing-room and I knew a few of the lads, but I didn't know them all because I hadn't been playing that long. Gerry Armstrong was playing for Antrim; I didn't know him at the time but I was making my debut and I remember it being talked about.

I was going over, back and forward to Celtic around that time, in the holidays or whenever I could get off work. I used to travel over from Belfast to Glasgow, and I'd get picked up by Jock Stein or Sean Fallon, a Sligo man. They put me up in a hotel and I remember going to training and then playing for the reserves. I did that on and off for six months, so I didn't train that much with Derry and I was mixing the two of them… the soccer and the gaelic.

WE TRAINED AT Ballinascreen in those days and Frankie had us running up and down banks at the side of the pitch. You had to get a partner on your back, run up with him and down again before we'd switch over. I was looking around for the lightest bloke I could see and that was Johnny O'Leary, but somebody else had bagged him. I ended up carrying Peter Stevenson up the bank. I was going nowhere near the bigger boys on the team. Tom McGuinness was that fit, he would've taken two men up that bank… he was a real athlete. Tom would've run all day, and after training he would do extra work on his fitness.

It was as professional as you wanted. We played forwards against backs at training and I remember Frankie stopping it to show us different things, tell us what we were doing and where we were going. He was a good manager and we all got on well with him. We were fit and we were very, very together.

We never travelled to any of the games by bus; we travelled in cars driven by GAA men from your area who'd take you to games. Frank Donaghy from Dungiven would pick us up… me, Mickey Lynch, Fintan McCloskey and Jude Hargan when he was on the panel. Liam Hinphey would be there, he was always involved with the North Derry lads.

Frank had a big Merc and it had a big boot, but we didn't need much room. We only had to bring our boots… I remember the socks, shorts and the kit all being hung up for us when we got there.

There was another car load that came from Derry city with Tom McGuinness, Johnny O'Leary, Mark McFeely and Frankie Treanor.

In our car, we always had the craic on the road and I'm sure it was the same with all the other boys coming from all the other parts of Derry. They used to call us the Banagher boys. Peter Stevenson, we'd sometimes pick him up and he'd laugh and ask how the Banagher boys were getting on. There was always plenty of banter.

WE PLAYED ARMAGH in the first round of the championship. I don't remember too much about that game. Next up was Monaghan and it took us two games to get over them.

Looking back at the first game, they were a big, strong side and they put themselves about. Going into the replay, I looked around and thought it was going to be another battle but it wasn't as tough as the first game. In those days, it was about going out and always needing to do your best. That was my mantra, I always went out to do my best.

Frankie Kearney would be on at us to get the pressure on and get the ball into the forwards as quickly as we could. Then, if we beat our opponents and turned them, nobody would catch us. Derry, in those days, the one thing they had was pace and had it in certain areas.

Tom McGuinness was a fielder and he had pace… they all had. It was a great team. We had Johnny O'Leary, Brendan Kelly, Mickey Moran, Kevin Teague, Eugene Laverty, Laurence Diamond and Adrian McGuckin.

I looked at Monaghan… and then you look around and see Seamus Lagan, Anthony McGurk and the big boys and you'd just think, *They'll protect me.* I had just turned 18. I felt confident they'd be able to mind me… and Mickey Lynch thought the same way.

IF YOU EVER see the photo of that Ulster final with Down, I had a bad cut on my left hand. I was working at the time as a cutter in Desmond's factory and I sliced my finger. Thankfully, Seamus Gormley's sister, Eithne, was a nurse and she bandaged it up for me and it held up. I didn't want any stitches in it. It happened on the Friday, but I didn't want to go to the doctors or the hospital, and I didn't tell Frankie until I got to Clones.

One thing Frankie told us, and he said to Anthony McGurk when he was getting the toss… was to play towards the board, the scoreboard end. And not the other way, the other way there is nothing to shoot at. The people behind the goals, you could see them. At the other end, there were a couple of trees and nothing to shoot at.

It started well for us and I scored a goal after two minutes; it was Sean O'Connell who got the ball around the edge of the square and he fed me.

I remember myself and Mickey Lynch, we knew each other well and we had things we did in the club team. If I shouted for the ball, he'd give it to me; there were no questions asked and if I saw Mickey going, it was the same… I'd just give him the ball.

Mickey, he was as strong as a horse. He got Man of the Match and all of his five points came from play, all at the end of hard worked moves.

After I scored the goal, it settled the nerves a little bit. It was the warmest day I have ever known in Clones. There were no such things as drink breaks or oranges at half-time. Looking back, all the players did well to get up the sets of steps and into the upper changing rooms in Clones.

From Derry to Clones, we'd time to chat about who would be picking each other up. Mr Hinphey always called me 'McElhinney' and he'd ask who'd be picking me up and I said I didn't know… probably the closest Down player.

There was banter all the time and we'd take it into the dressing-room. Before the game, Frankie would be sitting there and go over a few things with you. He'd tell me I would be picked up by Brendan Sloan today… and Sean O'Connell, you'll be picked up by Dan McCartan. Frankie, he'd go around telling us things and he would test your brain to see how you'd figure it out.

It is not the same as it is now. We had a plan and the plan was to get the ball to Sean O'Connell… and for me, Mickey Lynch and Johnny O'Leary to feed off him. It was up to Tom McGuinness and Eugene Laverty at midfield, to get it in to Sean. He must've been nearly 40 and it was about getting it into the big man; we called him 'The Master' as he was a schoolteacher.

We had Brendan Kelly, who was a free-taker, but we just tried to play to our strengths.

You had McGuiness, Laverty, behind that was Anthony McGurk, behind him was Tom Quinn and then goalkeeper John Somers. When you look down through the middle of the team, you had a group of players that weren't going to give up. There is a photograph of me looking at Anthony McGurk and he was pumped up, trying to get everybody going. I am looking at him... he was shouting something. He was a leader and, in that team, the players around middle were leaders and all big club players.

Sean O'Connell was one of the most skilful players I saw. He knew where the ball was going. At 38, he didn't need pace, he had the craft.

Dan McCartan would try and horse or batter you, but it never happened with Sean O'Connell, he was scared of Sean. I am sure they played against each other before; he'd have been scared of Sean because if you hit a ball into him, he made it stick.

He was 20 years older than me, and boy could he turn a game. Two or three years before that, I remember him playing for Ballerin and he made things look so easy. He had a great footballing brain. Frankie would go easy on him and he wouldn't have been doing much training. He would be practicing free-kicks. I remember that... and he didn't want Sean carrying anyone up that bank at Ballinascreen.

I THINK WE all realised it when we beat Down in the final, we knew an All-Ireland could be coming.

When we won the game, I couldn't believe how many people were on the field... Derry had won something big again. I couldn't believe going up the steps to get the cup and seeing all the fans there, people who followed Derry for years. If you ask them, they probably thought there was something big coming. There were neighbours from Banagher and Park, Ballerin, Glack, Derry City... there were two city men on the team.

When we went up to receive the cup, we got a standing ovation and Mickey Lynch thoroughly deserved Man of the Match, he would've run through a brick wall for Derry.

For the support, there was a huge crowd, it wasn't all-ticket like now... in those days everybody got through a hole in the fence.

We won three Ulster titles in six years. When you look back on it, Kerry and Dublin had great teams, and there weren't many counties that won All-Irelands. You could count on one hand the teams coming through in the 70s... Tyrone and Donegal were nowhere to be seen.

That Dublin team, we thought we were fit but they had some class players, their forwards were better than us. The Derry backs did as well as they could, but looking back we could've done different things... but we had a go, and that was it.

MY ALL STAR nomination must've arrived through the post. Frank McHenry, the Banagher manager, came to me and told me I was nominated.

I went down to Dublin with Anthony McGurk and Peter Stevenson, and it was the first time I ever had to wear a dickie bow... that was shock number one.

Sean O'Connell was with us as a replacement All Star; it was a great trip and we were staying with Irish families. We played games in New York, San Francisco and Los Angeles.

Shock number two was the fact that I was among superstars. Eddie Keher and Brian Cody were there, the best players in Ireland were all there... and I was one of them.

I was shocked to get one. I played pretty well in the Ulster final. I didn't do too bad in the semi-final. To be honest, there were a lot of better players around at the time. Mickey Lynch scored five points from play in the Ulster final and never got an All Star. I don't know how they did it, but it's in the history books now.

I enjoyed my time. If you said to me now, what would I change... I probably could've stuck to playing GAA.

There was something else I wanted to do, so I went for it. I could've failed at the soccer, but I played over 300 games for four clubs, and I played six international games. In my mind, I didn't fail.

If I had stuck at the gaelic, things could've turned out different, you don't know. I played for Gortin and Craigbane as well as Banagher, you could write a book about that in itself.

I enjoyed playing sport and that's me. It's not like nowadays that you're not allowed to play for your club.

After a county game, we were dying to get home and play for our club. You used to enjoy going to Aghabrack sports and playing seven-a-side. Then we'd get ham sandwiches and a bottle of Fanta. It was just great, we'd travel for miles to get playing football… anywhere.

It was different… and it's a different era now. It is not fully professional, but is very *professional* nowadays.

I couldn't say enough about that Derry team of 1975. There was a great togetherness and a terrific atmosphere.

There were people who never get mentioned… boys like Gabriel Bradley and Kevin Teague. They were all there when we had to pull it out of the bag against Down and Monaghan in the replay. All the boys stood up and were counted. Frankie oversaw it all, he was a great organiser. He was married to a girl who lived half a mile up the road from me in Dreen… Mena Devine.

Mam would say Frankie Kearney is on the phone and he'd say, 'Gerry, you will get picked up at Park Bridge at half 12 and don't be late, wee Donaghy is picking you up'.

He'd go up to Park houses to pick up Mickey Lynch… then Fintan McCloskey, then Peter Stevenson… and Liam Hinphey. It was all done by a phone call, there were no messages on mobile phones likes it is now.

Then he'd put up notices and he'd never tell you the team until an hour, or an hour and a half, before the game, but you always had an inkling. The boys that were marking the forwards in training, they wouldn't be playing.

The squads weren't very big then, we'd have had around 24 men. They were great times. The 70s were good, so were the 80s… and, thankfully, Derry won the All-Ireland in the 90s.

99

BRENDAN KELLY
(& ANTHONY McGURK)

DERRY 0-22 ★ CAVAN 1-16 (AET)
Ulster SFC Final Replay
St Tiernach's Park, Clones
JULY 25, 1976

★ **DERRY:** J Somers; L Murphy, T Quinn, P Stevenson; G O'Loughlin, **A McGurk** (0-1), M Moran (0-1); T McGuinness (0-1), L Diamond; **B Kelly (0-8)**, M Lynch (0-5), F McCloskey (0-3); G McElhinney (0-2), C Grieve, J O'Leary (0-1). **Subs:** E Laverty for Diamond, S O'Connell for Grieve, G Bradley for O'Loughlin.

★ **CAVAN:** A Elliott; P Tinnelly, D Dalton, E McGowan; S Leddy, F Dolan, P McGill; O Leddy (0-1), D Meade; C O'Keefe, O Brady (0-2), O Martin (0-2); G Cusack (0-1), S Duggan (0-7), J Dwyer (1-3). **Subs:** G O'Reilly for Dalton, JJ Martin for McGill, J Carroll for S Leddy, A King for Cusack.

66

I WON ULSTER with Derry minors in 1969 and '70. We lost the All-Ireland final to Cork the first year and that was followed by Kerry beating us in the semi-final the following year.

I had played for the under-21s but didn't initially get into the senior team because I decided to head across to America in 1974, where I was playing for Longford.

I went out with a few boys from around home. All I had was a duffle bag. In it, were a pair of boots, a pair of socks and underwear. We were standing in John F Kennedy Airport at about half one in the morning and this boy tapped me on the

THE ACTION

★★★★★

DERRY WENT THE extra mile to retain the Anglo Celt Cup thanks to a Man of the Match display from Anthony McGurk, and a combined 13 points from sharpshooters Brendan Kelly and Mickey Lynch.

Cavan forced the replay courtesy of a late and controversial goal in the drawn game when Peter Stevenson kicked home a dubious penalty won by Eugene Laverty.

With the lead changing hands 10 times, the replay was every bit as well contested. Larry Diamond bossed midfield early on before John Dwyer's goal levelled matters, and it always looked like a game going to the wire.

McGuinness, Lynch and McElhinney were on target as Derry led 0-8 to 1-2 by half-time. Kelly hit two points and Lynch looked to have won the game in normal time, only for Cavan to work a quick kick-out to JJ Martin before Dwyer pointed and the game was heading for extra-time.

McElhinney came deep and substitute Eugene Laverty also stepped up to the plate, with McGurk stamping his authority on the game as Derry pushed two points clear at half-time in extra-time. Kelly and O'Leary pointed for Derry, but when Cavan staged a comeback, it took Lynch's fifth of the afternoon to clinch victory. There were appeals for a Cavan penalty in the closing stages, but referee Gerry Fagan awarded a free out and Derry breathed a sigh of relief.

Derry's improvement from the replay cemented their position as Kings of Ulster.

★★★★★

shoulder to come and play for them. I had no idea who he was, but he said he'd get us work… and we were started work by half six that morning.

I had played for Derry against Antrim in one of the cup competitions, but when I came back from America in '74 I played in the National League that year. We played Galway down in Ballinascreen's Dean McGlinchey Park. They were in the All-Ireland final the year before and had two All Stars in their half-back line. For Derry, it was myself, Brian Ward and Mickey Moran in the half-forward line.

I can remember going for a job interview in St Mark's up in Twinbrook before the 1975 Ulster final with Down. One of the priests on the interview panel could see from my application form I had played minor football and I was starting out on the Derry senior team.

He started to talk about the match and was asking me who was going to win it, and I said it was going to be Derry.

He asked me how I was so confident? I said Sean O'Neill and Dan McCartan were playing for Down, but I also asked him if he had ever heard of Brendan Kelly or Mickey Lynch or Gerry McElhinney? I told him that's our half-forward line.

We had a good side but the problem was Down always having the upper hand over us. That may have been a factor for others, but it wasn't a factor to me. At minor or under-21, Down had never beaten us. Myself and the six or seven of us who came off that team, we had no worries.

I remember Malachy McAfee in the dressing-room. I was pleasantly surprised how relaxed I was and I was looking at McAfee. To me, he was a great footballer but I couldn't believe it, he could hardly tie his laces with nerves.

I had no fear of Down. I would've been okay with nerves. Myself and Gerry O'Loughlin would've sat beside each other. He was another cool customer and you looked across at players like Anthony McGurk and the Damper (Peter Stevenson). McGuinness was another boy who was nervous but he was a great footballer when he went out and got going.

It was brilliant playing on that team. Frankie Kearney was the manager and I remember back to that Galway game, earlier in the year. The first thing he did was lift £10 a man and told us it was 8/1 against Derry to win the Ulster final, but we were going to won it. He put on the bet, and we were comfortable enough with it.

Everybody was there training, but when I was on the minor side, you'd have looked at the Derry senior team coming out and kicking the ball up into the air on a good day at training… and if it was a bad day, they wouldn't.

I remember Mick Lawless saying that's why we were going to win the minor All-Ireland and the seniors were going to lose the first round.

That didn't happen under Kearney. You either trained or you weren't there. Frankie, Sean O'Connell, Patsy Breen, Seamus Kelly and Liam Hinphey… that was the management team.

Kearney was the organiser and was doing everything right. It was the first time we got the blazers. We were the black and tans. He designed the Derry badge and had it sewn onto the jacket. We were a unit.

Losing the '75 All-Ireland semi-final… we lost the match but I had played well. They were all household names. I remember coming off thinking Robbie Kelleher is not that good of a footballer. I thought he was alright, but was happy enough with my game.

Dublin beat us and when we all walked off, we thought we could've learned from it and come back again.

WE WERE SO far behind in professionalism at that time compared to Dublin and Kerry. We weren't in the park at all as regards training.

I remember being down at the Rose of Tralee in 1976, after Kerry had given us an awful hammering in the All-Ireland semi-final. I got chatting to Mick O'Dwyer's bag man, Leo Griffin. He asked me about our preparation coming up to the game and when I told him we trained two nights a week, he told us that Kerry trained 16 times in the fortnight before they played that game.

In the first-half, we were one hundred percent… and also good 10 minutes into the second-half. After that, I knew we had no answer to Kerry and their fitness. They were training away, with Dublin and Kerry pushing each other on.

We were always within the kick of a ball from Dublin. They should never have won the '76 National League final against us… we had them destroyed in the first-half. I think we were leading 0-9 to 0-2 at one-point. Big Seamus Lagan caught the ball and turned around and hit the bar, and they went up and put it in the back of our net. From being seven points up, there was four points in it.

They talk about blanket defences now, but this was the first time I saw it. In the last two minutes, John Somers, our goalie, was the only man in the Derry half of the field. Everybody else was inside the 50-yard line. I remember coming outside to try and make a run, but they had it closed up.

The league was being played on a north and south basis. We always played against Galway and Mayo, and that was a big disadvantage going into the All-Ireland series. All we read about in the papers was about these great footballers in the other teams… Kerry and Dublin. When you met them, a lot of them were just the same as ourselves.

After winning Ulster in 1975, we set out to do it again in '76. We had two games to get over Cavan in the final and I really enjoyed those matches. When I was young, Michael O'Hehir was commentating on the games and he'd be talking about the 'Men of Breffni' and it made the hair stand on the back of your neck.

You'd have been getting your tea after mass and waiting to three o'clock to hear O'Hehir commentating on the 'Men of Breffni' and thinking it would be great to play against those boys. This was in the late 50s, and he was commentating on Jim McDonnell, Hugh Barney O'Donohoe and Charlie Gallagher. Then there was Jim McKeever, Patsy Breen, Sean O'Connell and those boys on the Derry team.

Now, I was getting out on the field against the 'Men of Breffni'. Kerry or Dublin didn't mean anything to me… Cavan was the team.

We played Tyrone in the Ulster minor final in 1969 at Casement Park. Down were playing Cavan in the senior game and Down were All-Ireland champions the year before. I remember going in to get togged out and stopping at the Cavan dressing-room, looking in the door and seeing the blue jerseys.

There was a boy making a speech. You talk about Ian Paisley talking… you felt like going in and lifting one of the jerseys, and going out with them. It was a magnificent speech. By the time we got changed and went out, Cavan were hammering Down in the senior final that followed our game.

I always had a great affinity with Cavan, the blue and white jersey… the 'Men of Breffni'.

In the drawn game, I thought we had it won. I remember punching a ball over the bar down at the lower end. That put us in front, but they took it up the field and Stevie Duggan put it over the bar. We were also lucky to get out of it. It was one of the games, they could've lost it or we could've lost.

THAT REPLAYED FINAL was a day I will always remember for a whole lot of different things. We stopped at the Four Seasons and had tea before the match.

Then you go up the hill in Clones, and I remember getting out of the car and seeing a sea of blue and white and red and white. It was just a really hot day and people were coming over and slapping you and saying, 'Right, Neilly you're going to do it today'.

Gerry O'Loughlin and myself were in the car. You were meeting neighbours wishing you well and it was a lovely feeling. The atmosphere was great. When we walked down the dressing-room steps, it was a sunny day and the pitch was nice and hard. It was an awesome feeling.

The only time I worried about the favourites' tag was the year before with the Down supremacy. I had no worries against Cavan. Beating Down, the chip was off the shoulder and it helped the older boys who had never won against them.

I remember Derry playing Down in earlier years and watching Colm McAlarney running through; we were up in the stands and couldn't believe it. There was *nobody* running through Derry this time. You had the Damper, McGurk, O'Loughlin… you didn't run through them, you had to work your way through.

I remember looking over at Paddy McGill to see what size of legs he had. I was expecting these giants from Breffni. He was a tough man, and Enda McGowan, who would've been marking me as well.

The tackles were brilliant, there was no lying down like in soccer. If you lay down, you had a reason to lie down. That game went on… pounding on and this is why I remember the game because it really turned into *my* game in the last five minutes.

We were getting beat by two points and went on the attack. It was broken up and cleared down the field. McGurk got the ball and he could've been 30 or 40 yards from our goals. As soon as I saw him looking up, I pointed to where I wanted it.

McGurk gave me his usual exquisite pass. He put the head down and kicked it as high and hard as he could down towards me.

I remember coming onto it and seeing the ball bouncing, and thought it was going over my head. I remember stretching with my fingertips. It stuck. I came down and sold my dummy and the man just pulled me down. I was around the 50-yard line. It was a bit far out for me. I remember everybody in around the square and thinking this has to go over the bar.

I started to wave at Sean O'Connell to come across. I was linking his bald spot up with the black spot on the bar. Kearney always said aim for the black spot but two things to aim at was better.

O'Connell was panicking, thinking I was kicking it in to him but I told him after that I was lining his bald spot up with the black spot. To this day, I never saw the ball going over the bar, but just saw the red and white flags going up. That left us a point down and time moving on.

I got the ball on the 14-yard line, next the sideline. I was very far out and I thought I had to go out the field to get a bit of room. All I could hear was 'Stick on the left foot'. There might've only been two men, but it seemed like the whole Cavan side were coming in front of me. I cut inside and went across, sold my dummy… and the boy bought it and when I went to bounce the ball, I was pulled down.

That was a big, big moment. Setting the ball down, I could hear boys shouting 'Come on Neilly, you can score it' and remember two wee Cavan girls shouting… 'Miss it… miss it!'

Putting the ball down, looking up, it was a narrow angle. The way I was thinking, there might be another attack. I said I had to do what I did in the park up in Ballinascreen… and kick it over the bar.

I knew I could do it, but doing it was a completely different thing. I took a big breath. The difference in this from the one from 50 yards out… when I hit this, I knew I had scored it. I lifted my head up and I could see the ball going through and the Derry flags going up. I thought the game was over, but the ball was kicked out and it was put down the middle of the field.

Big Ollie Leddy was in the middle of the field. He was about six foot three and I remember thinking the ball was going to break. Nobody was punching the ball; everyone went up to catch. It broke straight to me. I couldn't believe it; I just bounced the ball and went past my man and saw a gap. I went straight at the gap.

All I could see was the Cavan full-back standing on his own. At that point, Mickey Lynch went on my left side. I bounced the ball, headed for the Cavan man and punched it to Mickey. I didn't see the point, but I had my fist in the air. That put us a point in front, and we thought the game was over.

I turned and by the time I got out to my man, the ball was going down the field. John Dwyer, the last man in Ireland you wanted to see, had the ball and kicked it over the bar. Aidan Elliott was in goals for Cavan. I am wondering did he hit the kick-out from behind the goals. I don't know how it got out. I asked more people and nobody could tell me.

We were hanging about chatting about it all after full-time, but Kearney was shouting not to worry about it because there was extra-time.

Mickey Lynch was there… and that's when I knew we'd win it. I knew it when he was on our side. He was some player. I wouldn't have wanted him playing for Cavan. I looked at Lynch and said to myself, *Brendan, you get behind Lynch and pass the ball to him every time you get it.* And that's what I did.

I didn't go over the halfway line at all, I let Lynch run my corridor. He was a great athlete. He was like a greyhound… but one of those big dogs, like a St Bernard. He was well built and he could fly. He absolutely destroyed Cavan in extra time. His man Ollie Brady had no mission at all of getting near him. It was half-time in extra time before they realised what was happening, and we had control of the game. We knew we had it. Lynch was running riot; they could do nothing with him.

IT WAS AN even better winning feeling than the year before. It was Cavan, who I longed to play against… it was back-to-back, and the apprehension of 1975 was gone. You wanted to move on with your own level of football.

It was a completely different feeling when we went to the Four Seasons after it. Even among the supporters, it seemed to be bigger or that was my interpretation. It was just a special day.

That first day we played Cavan in the drawn final, I had just reclaimed the field where our house is now. I sewed it out in corn on the Saturday with a fiddle… all 10 acres, going across and back. When I think about it now, it was a very hot day and it was silly. It would never happen now.

I didn't do it before the second day, because Enda McGowan hit me a great shoulder and I knew it in my legs for a while after it, and I knew the reason for it.

Those days against Cavan, they are memories until the day I die.

★★★★★

ANTHONY McGURK

66

MY FIRST INVOLVEMENT with Derry was as a minor in 1966 and '67. Derry had won the All-Ireland minor in 1965 and I was fortunate to be selected for the under-21 team in 1968, when we won the All-Ireland. After that, I joined the senior panel. When we won the Ulster Championship in 1970, I played in the first two games against Tyrone and Cavan. I came on in the final against Antrim when Malachy McAfee got injured after 10 minutes, going in at half-back. I also came on as a sub against Kerry in the All-Ireland semi-final that year.

My main memories of that year and the years that followed, I suppose, were of how they were unproductive. I think Derry had the potential to win three or four Ulsters, if not All-Irelands, around that time. Offaly won an All-Ireland in 1971 and '72, and we had beaten them in the under-21 final in 1968. So, there was an expectation that we could achieve what they did.

We were a big physical team, with some excellent fielders of the ball, and some very good players throughout the forwards and backs. At that stage, we were competing with – and on most occasions beating – all other teams in Ireland, except when it came to the championship.

From 1970 onwards, we had opportunities to win All-Irelands because we did not fear any other team in Ireland and had the capacity to beat them. Things later changed when Dublin won the All-Ireland in 1975, and Kerry the year after. The physical stakes then got a lot higher and they were the two major powers in Ireland.

To go back a few years, my minor career was not particularly successful, though I did win a MacRory Cup with St Columb's in Derry, where I was a boarder. My own career changed when I went to study at Queen's University and bought contact lenses. I am very short-sighted and would've played in glasses when I was a minor, if I had been allowed to.

Then it got to the stage where I had to leave them at the side of the pitch and play without them. I hated playing in the 'carnivals' because the games were usually finishing when it was starting to get dark. I would've been asking who had the ball, who had scored... or if the play was going in a certain direction.

In my first year at university, I got a grant of £120 a term and I immediately spent £40 on a set of contact lenses. I kept wearing them for three or four days just to get used to them – even though my eyes were watering – but it made a massive difference to my football, the enjoyment of it and my life in general. It helped my reaction in going for the ball, seeing where it was coming from when it was kicked. Before that, I was reliant on chance... especially during the 'carnivals' and on those dark nights.

AT THAT TIME, the Derry team was beating most other teams in the National League that were contending and winning All-Irelands. When it came to the championship, it was a different matter – getting out of Ulster was problematic. There were always a number of teams in contention. The remnants of the Down team of the 1960s was still there... Sean O'Neill, Colm McAlarney and a few others. Cavan always had a strong team, and Donegal had a good period at the start of the 70s too, winning in 1972.

Derry was a match for all of them. I can remember 1971... we played Down in the Ulster final in Casement Park and the score was 4-15 to 4-11. They beat us and should've gone on and won the All-Ireland that year, but missed out against Galway. Every year, we set out hoping to go all the way. It was more of a lottery then than it is now, with a lot of teams in contention and no back-door opportunity if you failed.

Back then, we competed successfully over a number of years in the Wembley Tournament. The four All-Ireland semi-finalists travelled to England to play exhibition matches – one match was on the Saturday in Wembley, and the other was on the Sunday at London GAA's headquarters in New Eltham. We won those games on several occasions.

Breaking the mould and winning a first title is difficult, and people will say it requires belief that you can actually win. Then you can make it a habit. When I started watching football, Down were one of the lesser lights in Ulster. Derry won Ulster in 1958, and Down were nowhere. Then they became prominent in the mid-60s. Once they had a number of titles under their belt, they had the belief that they could beat anyone.

I am friendly with Sean O'Neill, and we meet for the odd coffee. He epitomised that confidence and belief. Down weren't fond of Kerry and a number of other southern teams, and believed there was nobody better than themselves. It wasn't that they were any better than any other Down teams that came before or after, but they had fantastic belief in their ability. Once they got their first All-Ireland win, they were confident they could compete with any other team in Ireland and other counties started to fear their reputation. A lot of sport is about confidence and most teams need one success to instil that. However, a balance needs to be struck between expectation and keeping your feet firmly on the ground.

When I think of our team that won Ulster in 1975 and '76, I feel that we should also have won in '77 against Armagh. Armagh won't agree with me, but we were much too confident in that match. Some of our players went to America – including Mickey Moran and Brendan Kelly – and we expected to win Ulster without them, and that they would return for the All-Ireland semi-final. We had beaten Armagh the year before. In 1977, we could've won three in-a-row, but we messed up.

ANY TEAM I was selected for, I would've played in any position; it didn't matter. I just liked playing and have fond memories of those I played with. When Derry needed a half-back, I was half-back, and when Derry needed a full-forward or a half-forward, I was happy to go there. I even played in midfield for a while.

It was easy for me to adapt to play on either side of the defence because I could kick with both feet. When I was young, I was right-handed and right-footed. My father was left-handed and left-footed, and he bought me a plastic ball when I was three or four. He held my right foot until I kicked with the left. When I started playing football, I wasn't massively accurate but I could've kicked it easily with either foot.

For Derry seniors, I played everywhere expect in goals, although I did 'play' there once, in 1996 during Brian Mullins' first game as manager, when I was a selector. We played Sligo in a challenge match and the one 'keeper on our panel got injured. Mullins told me to go into goals and I ended up playing there. It was my last ever game… aged 47!

The first All Star I got, in 1973, was at corner-forward and I was lucky to get it as there were many other very good footballers about who played in that position. All Stars are great, I am glad I won them and I had a great time in

America, but they are a bit of a lottery. It's a bit like politics in that there are a number of Ulster journalists who rightly support their own people against other players from other provinces.

Few southern GAA journalists were coming up to see Ulster matches and there was little coverage of the game on television. The Ulster journalists would've punted for three or four players. It wasn't about positions – they'd have slotted you in somewhere.

I was a replacement All Star in 1972 and I played really well out in America, but at the end of the day they were still just challenge matches. There is obviously a bit of pride at stake – and usually an odd row – but it's not a true test. The true tests are the championship matches. However, it did get me noticed by the journalists who were there. My second All Star was at centre half-back two years later. That was my position for both Derry and Lavey at that stage.

IN 1975, DERRY had a good athletic team and had done well in the National League. We beat Armagh in the first round of the championship but nearly lost in the semi-final against Monaghan and needed a replay. We played Down in the final and it was typical the Ulster Championship; sometimes you could've gone out early, but we got through and won reasonably comfortably. We then lost to Dublin in the All-Ireland semi-final by four or five points.

Looking forward to the following season – 1976 – we should've won the National League that year. We beat Galway in a play-off to make the semi-finals and our manager, Frankie Kearney, placed me at corner-back in that match. We won and beat Cork in the semi-final, but when it came to the final against Dublin, I pulled a hamstring in the week leading up to it. I went out bandaged and thought I was alright, but I wasn't anywhere near well enough to be playing.

From then on, I had a problem with hamstrings because I had a tendency to come back too early. I just wanted to play and was happy to get strapped up. I was probably one of the first players to get an injection for pain relief to allow me to play, but that wasn't the right thing for my recovery. From then until I finished with Lavey, I wore a big blue bandage to support the hamstrings.

Frankie Kearney was in charge around that time. The Derry campaign was more organised and the training was that bit tougher. Sean O'Connell was taking a lot of the fitness training – even though he was playing that year. He played very little at training but was still capable of a big performance on match day.

We'd have been running up the banks around Ballinascreen pitch and started to go to the sand hills in Portstewart, running up and down there and doing a lot of work on sand. In the 60s, they reckoned all the best long and middle-distance runners were from New Zealand and Australia, and they trained on sand. You have to take shorter steps and it increases your accelerating power.

It was totally different to now. I would imagine there is a bit more bonding and camaraderie nowadays. I would've picked up Seamus Lagan on the way, the Bellaghy boys would've joined us… and we'd have gone to training, and afterwards into Timoney's Café in Draperstown for a pint of milk and a salad. Then it was back into the car and away on home. There wasn't the habit of going to pubs, but there was the odd night out. Now clubs have clubhouses and you meet there. Back then, you were lucky if you'd changing rooms, and once you were changed, you were away home so there wasn't as much interaction among the players.

The mid-70s training regime differed drastically from when I started playing with Derry. Back then, you got changed and went out onto the pitch, where you kicked in for the first 10 or 15 minutes. Then you did a couple of laps, a bit of sprinting and then a game of backs against forwards. We finished up with a jog around the pitch and that was it. We'd have been out on a Tuesday and Thursday – twice a week max – and we'd never have thought about a Saturday.

Frankie was a master of organisation and that's what he brought to the team. If we were going somewhere, he knew exactly the time… where you were going, where you were staying and what you were doing. We'd go out on Saturday for a kickabout to get boys together, thinking and talking about the match. This was the beginning of proper focusing on matches.

Seamus Kelly, Liam Hinphey and Sean O'Connell were no different. They were all teachers, and O'Connell had the experience from playing and knew what to do. There was a bit more training because teams were looking more at their fitness levels then than in the 60s and early 70s. That arrived with the Dublin and Kerry teams of that period, who'd be training four or five times a week, which was unheard of. Mick O'Dwyer had a young team and he gave them great confidence. He was in charge of the All Star teams when I played and there was nothing different about his training methods. He had a different set of players to work with, but there was nothing novel in his coaching style.

Looking back, we won the 1976 Ulster Championship matches comfortably, apart from Cavan in the final, where we needed a replay. We should've won the first day but also could've lost it. We gave away a goal and a few silly points. It was the same the second day: we should've won the match and then nearly threw it away. They took it to extra time and then, fortunately, we pulled away.

The reason the replayed final was significant in my career was because we won two in-a-row and nobody had done that in recent times. I played well that day and got Man of the Match in both games – the drawn match and the replay. It was a different story in the All-Ireland semi-final against Kerry. We were a point up at half-time, but they took off in the second-half and beat us well.

We were a mature team then. We had been together for two or three years. We had mostly been used to winning over that period. We didn't win in 1974, but we went well in the National League. We didn't fear any team, and we had the confidence and desire to go further. We had very good players that would've got their place on any team in Ireland. Mickey Lynch was flying and Gerry McElhinney was very good. Laurence Diamond and Tom McGuinness were there in the middle of the field, and Eugene Laverty had come in. They were big men. Brendan Kelly was an exceptionally good forward and Johnny O'Leary was a flier, so there was a good balance. John Somers was as good a 'keeper as ever, and Gerry O'Loughlin and Peter Stevenson brought all their experience to the table.

I FEEL WE missed our best chance of All-Ireland success in 1977. You think of the foolish things we did that you wouldn't do now. We went and watched Roscommon and Galway in the Connacht final, before we even played in the Ulster final. This was the year to come through because we were to play the Connacht winners and the thinking was that we would be more or less guaranteed an All-Ireland final.

That is what we were looking at, but everybody took their eyes off the match at hand in looking ahead to the All-Ireland final. We reckoned we'd coast through against Roscommon from Connacht and didn't consider the challenge of Armagh. We were too confident… that's my story. I have no regrets. I would've loved to have won an All-Ireland, but I am a very lucky person in football and every way. I won All-Ireland under-21, Sigerson and Railway Cup medals. In the latter stage of my career, I won an All-Ireland Club and I have three championships, so I am luckier than a lot of other players.

I did think we had the capacity to win Sam in the early 70s – it would've been easier than in the mid-70s. I am not saying it was a better team – it was totally different to the 1975 and '76 team, which was more athletic.

I would love to be back in my twenties again and would love to play the game now because I think I could play it. There is more up and down the field but you have less marking to do, to some extent. You are setting your stall out at the '50' and then it is a matter of breaking tackles. I would like that, but I can't watch it.

I am not a fan of the current game at all but I would love to play it.

DERMOT McNICHOLL

ST PATRICK'S MAGHERA 2–10 ★ ABBEY CBS 0–8
MacRory Cup Final
Casement Park, Belfast
MARCH 13, 1983

★ **ST PATRICK'S:** D Kelly; D Quinn, J McGrath, P McGrellis; V McNicholl, P McCann, N Mullan; **D McNicholl**, D Dougan (0–2); G O'Kane, C McNicholl, J McGurk; C Rafferty, D Cassidy (1–1), R Scullion (1–7). **Sub:** D Mackle for Quinn.

★ **ABBEY:** D McCorry; A Magennis, P O'Neill, B Irvine; R Carroll (0–1), C McShane, J Carville; B Conlon, R O'Neill; D Kearney (0–2), DJ Kane (0–1), K McGurk; A Ruddy (0–3), C Rankin, M McEvoy (0–1). **Sub:** A Toner for Rankin.

66

I WON A Corn na nÓg medal in second year, but the following year I was messing about at school. I wasn't allowed to play on the team, so my football in third year was then played with the MacRory team.

We beat the Abbey in that 1980 MacRory final and, looking back on it now, I was pretty strong and had the ability to be able to hold my own with players older than me. I must admit I did find it difficult playing football and fully getting to know boys in sixth form. I'd be travelling to the games and, afterwards, when the games were over, these guys were going out, whereas, me… I'd be heading home.

I just put my head down and played away at the football. The MacRory Cup in our school was built on the craic you'd have in the sixth form centre, in the library and walking around the school.

THE ACTION

★★★★★

MAGHERA CAME FROM five points down to storm their way to back-to-back MacRory Cup final wins over rivals Abbey.

The Derry side edged Abbey by a point in the 1982 final that ended in controversy after an appeal over captain Martin Tully playing the final despite being sent off in the semi-final. Officials exonerated the skipper, bringing spice into the following year, but Maghera were hungry to put the result beyond any doubt.

It took them 17 minutes to get to grips with the game, but they ran out even more convincing winners than the scoreline suggests.

Damian Cassidy had fisted a Dermot McNicholl lob to the net midway through the first-half, only for the goal to be disallowed despite Cassidy appearing to have run into the square.

Ace attacker Rory Scullion hit two points to level matters and when he hammered to the net, after a Colm Rafferty pass with 12 minutes to go, Maghera were on their way to a 1-8 to 0-5 lead.

Derek Kearney notched points for the Newry side, but another fisted goal from Cassidy – that stood this time – sealed the deal for the champions, who had captain Dermot McNicholl at the heart of all they created.

★★★★★

It was about the camaraderie you had with the players in your year group, and I was thrust into a group with players who were three or four years older than me. There were times when we were coming home from matches and boys would've pulled me down to the back of the bus for a bit of craic.

I just trained away, played the matches and it was the same when I got the call from Matt Trolan for the Derry minors. I came in at the Ulster final and the All-Ireland time of the season, like a fish out of water. I remember travelling down for the All-Ireland final and never broke breath to anyone, it was surreal because you didn't know anybody.

In 1981, I was out with injury after dislocating my shoulder in an under-16 final with Glenullin... I was out for three or four months. I didn't come into the MacRory team until around the semi-final time, as the competition was finishing up. We were beaten by St Colman's Newry that year and they had a great team... players like Greg Blaney, Paul Hazard and Paul Skelton, boys who were all Armagh and Down minors.

I WANTED TO get to St Pat's Maghera after primary school. If I didn't get there, that would've been a disaster on my part... I just wanted to go there. Adrian McGuckin had created that aura that if you played for St Pat's Maghera then you had a good chance of going on with the transition to county level, leading you on to play for the Derry seniors. It was a pathway many young players had in my time. I was lucky in that I had a pathway in Glenullin from underage with Danny McIlvar in charge and that moved on to Maghera school, and then county senior level.

Going into 1982, that was the start of me progressing with my own football. Before that, I was used as a half or a corner-forward. Now, I was in a midfield partnership with Danny O'Kane and we'd been midfield together in our Glenullin underage teams.

I started to really enjoy my football out there. You were given more opportunity to get involved in the games more, whereas in the forwards you were only as involved as the supply of ball you got.

At MacRory level, you were coming up against a lot of county players, and it was all county players you were coming up against. We beat Abbey 1-7 to 1-6 in the 1982 final. It was an intriguing game and the bar was set high for that final.

Colman's hadn't come through that year and we felt in '81 we had a team to win the Hogan, until they beat us in the MacRory.

We had quite a few of us back again in 1982 and to win that MacRory was an important one. We felt we had the players to push for the Hogan that year as well.

It was around that time when school games began to get more coverage from the media and I can remember Paddy O'Hara interviewing me for a final. You could sense the game was getting more respect, and more people were taking an interest in it. More boys wanted to come to Maghera because of the success we were having.

Colman's fell off for a few years, and Abbey came in. There were great rivalries. In that '82 final, they were ahead of us and it wasn't looking like we were going to win it. Everything was working for them, and nothing was going for us. I remember getting a scrappy goal and I don't even know how I scored it. I remember seeing a photo where I was being tackled at the top and at the bottom, by the goalkeeper and a defender. I was able to drop it onto my left foot and punt kick it into the net… it was the winning of the game.

When he was presented with the cup, our captain Martin Tully was told to enjoy it because it was going to Newry the following night. This all came from him being sent off at the tail end of our semi-final win over St Pat's Armagh, when there was a bit of a schmozzle. Martin went in to pull boys out and the referee came in and sent off the first two players he saw.

The referee said he sent off Martin Tully in the wrong, because he overreacted… that was his statement and that Martin Tully, as the Maghera captain, was trying to mediate.

Adrian never mentioned it and we knew nothing about it, so there was no real talk about Martin playing or not playing in the final. When it came around to the big day, Martin was togged out and was playing.

Looking back on it now, when they saw him lining out, Abbey would've been very angry and I would say it didn't help their preparations on the day, and what happened afterwards. I remember going into school the next day after the final and the chat was that a taxi was being sent up to Maghera and it was going to take the cup to Newry, because they were awarded the match as Martin was ineligible and had played the final.

When the whole chat around that started, our preparation for the Hogan Cup was a disaster, and Skibbereen beat us.

AT THAT TIME, the three colleges putting in a big push were ourselves, St Colman's and the Abbey. A rivalry was starting to develop and before a ball was kicked for the 1983 season, there was a feeling that we hadn't won the thing in '82. I am not even sure if we got medals or the school bought medals, but there was a feeling that we weren't being painted as winning the MacRory or getting the respect.

We went into that campaign always looking over our shoulders to see how the Abbey were getting on, and we stayed apart until the final. Then you had Val Kane and Adrian McGuckin involved with the teams, who were really strong characters. Looking back on it now… both teams had most of the same characters who remembered what happened the year before so there was serious pressure.

Adrian, for whatever reason, he took us out to train in Swatragh in the build-up to that final. You were getting out of class an hour earlier, to get us away from the hype in school or to get extra daylight. I remember us doing runs across Swatragh pitch and wondered why were we doing this just 10 or 12 days before a final. Adrian had us doing sprints, with the froth coming out of our mouths for that final. We were ready and Adrian brought in psychology before we even knew what he was doing.

All the finals back then were in Casement. I loved it and you were coming out below the stand and with the noise belting out, you just knew this was a special final.

You'd always have had a meeting on the Friday before a game and Adrian didn't build us up too much. He'd have gone through the importance of getting an electric start. Bit by bit, he went through what he expected from the full-back line and all the way through the team. He'd have picked out players on the other team that needed watching.

He didn't say too much to me and I remember thinking it was odd he didn't mention too much about my man. In other years, he'd have told me who I was marking to help me get my head around it. This final was different. On the day, when we were getting ourselves ready in the changing rooms and the jerseys were going out, I remember heading to the toilet and Adrian walking after me.

'Dermot, you are going to have to do something different today!' he told me, and that absolutely took the wind out of me. I was going to be marking Brian Conlon and when Adrian was saying this, I knew I was going to be in a game. It was the first time he had said something like that to me on a one-on-one. He was basically telling me that my man was every bit as good as I was.

I compare him to Gary Ablett, who played in the AFL. Brian was a Rolls Royce… he was a clean footballer; he could catch it and he had *everything*. When you ran into him, you knew all about it.

Antrim were playing a hurling match before it and the Ulster Colleges lined up the two MacRory teams inside the Casement Park tunnel, waiting on the hurlers to go back to the changing rooms. Anyone who played there will tell you how tight the tunnel was. Players were roaring at each other… there were pushing and shouldering. I was hitting DJ Kane with a shoulder, and he was hitting me back.

It was intense after what happened in 1982. This was happening, and there was screaming and I'm sure those hurlers were walking through and wondering what the hell was going on. I felt it was a set-up and they hoped there was going to be absolute carnage, but you just had to hold your discipline. This was before a ball was kicked. We didn't expect it and it was the worst thing that could've happened.

Paul McCann, God rest him, the veins were sticking out on his head. I don't know how the teams got out onto the field without somebody getting hurt. The 2-10 to 0-8 scoreline didn't reflect the game itself as we got the goals at good times.

Looking back on it all, for pure excitement, playing the game and why you were playing the game… it was to test yourself. A lot of the players now don't know what it is like to be left one-on-one in front of 3,000 or 4,000 people in Casement Park at a MacRory final… TV cameras, and you are on your own.

We were tested as individuals… me versus Brian Conlon. I'd love to have played against him in more games because we'd have brought the best out in each other. That's what sport entails. Now, the system will protect the weaknesses that a team has.

In those MacRory finals, you had situations when you were under the hammer for a long time. To me, that is the reason why I went to St Pat's and the reason why I wanted to play sport. You are testing yourself against the best and seeing how you can cope.

I remember playing an under-21 game against Antrim, when I scored 3-6. I could've picked that as my best game, but I wasn't even being marked. Looking back on it, that '83 MacRory final was my best ever game when I think of what gaelic football is about.

Adrian told me that I had to win that battle with Brian Conlon and if we were going to come through, we'd have to win that battle. If he'd said that to me on the Friday, I'd have been thinking of that and I mightn't have slept. When you think about it, that was good coaching from Adrian's point of view. Looking back on that game and the pressure for both schools, their honour and reputation were on the line.

When you pick a performance, it's not always about your best individual skill, it takes in everything. It's how you cope with the enormity of the task that is put in front of you.

I looked at the MacRory final and the serious pressure, I was only 15 or 16 at the time.

The pressure from school as a whole, everybody knew about the bad feeling between Abbey and ourselves at that time. I am sitting here at 57 years of age, and I am still able to talk about that. It was a game you just could not lose.

Winning as captain, it was absolutely brilliant and I often think of all those things Adrian did to motivate you. He always put the team up on the noticeboard on the Friday, no matter what the game was... a group game, a semi-final or final. It didn't matter, it would be written in the most beautiful writing.

Everyone was scrambling to see what the team was; it was creating a culture within the school and that's what he did, and I suppose it was a culture war we had with the Abbey.

WE WON THE MacRory again in 1984. Myself and DJ Kane ended up in Jordanstown on the same Sigerson panel. We trained together, but never broke breath to each other. The both of us were as thick as hell. Tommy Joe Farrell pulled us into a room and told us we weren't kicking ball for Jordanstown until it was sorted.

I won two Sigersons on the field with DJ, and another when him and his brother Val were managers, the same men we were up against in the MacRory Cup. Val was a very good manager and me and DJ, we are very close, as thick as thieves. Sitting here now, if I rang him now to come down and meet up, he'd be here in no time.

Back then, we were going toe-to-toe on the big MacRory days. Now, when I look back, college football helps you push on to play for the county. I was marking players like Stephen Mulvenna, Stephen Muldoon, Brian Conlon and Donal Durkin… I came across them all who went on to play for the county. I would never have come across them only for the college competition.

The grounding came from here, from Glenullin and Danny McIlvar. There's a wee hall across the Glen where it all started. He'd have us kicking ball, and it moved to school and from there to the county.

To me, you can never say you've played your best game. That's a fact. There is always a game in you if you are developing, but that statement from Adrian… 'looking for something different'… I will never forget that one.

BRIAN McGILLIGAN

DERRY 0-8 ★ MEATH 0-15
All-Ireland SFC Semi-Final
Croke Park, Dublin
AUGUST 23, 1987

★ **MEATH:** M McQuillan; R O'Malley, M Lyons, T Ferguson; K Foley, L Harnan, M O'Connell; L Hayes (0-1), G McEntee; D Beggy (0-1), J Cassells (0-2), PJ Gillic; C O'Rourke (0-3), B Stafford (0-4), B Flynn (0-4). **Sub:** F Murtagh for Cassells.

★ **DERRY:** D McCusker; HM McGurk, D Quinn, T Scullion; P McCormack, J Irwin (0-2), P McCann; P Murphy, **B McGilligan**; E Gormley (0-5), S Downey, D Barton; D Cassidy, D McNicholl, P Kealey (0-1) **Subs:** T McGuckin for McNicholl, M Bradley for McCann, P Mackle for McCormack.

66

FOOTBALL WOULDN'T HAVE been high on my radar at the start. I was handy enough at the hurling, and it was my number one game as far as I was concerned.

Maybe it was in my own head, but I was better at hurling and I enjoyed it far more. In Derry, the opportunities weren't there for you. If I had been in some of the other counties, even across in Antrim, I would've got a better run at it.

In my final year of minor, I was a sub with the Derry minors when Cork beat us in the 1981 All-Ireland football final. The manager said if there were changes to be made, I would be in the running. Cork blew Derry out of the water that day and they put other players on, but I didn't get a look in.

I had begun playing in goals for Dungiven minors at the start and I wasn't

THE ACTION

★★★★★

A MAN OF the Match performance from Brian McGilligan wasn't enough to pull Derry into an All-Ireland final, as Meath's inside trio shot the Royals to a first decider in 17 years. Colm O'Rourke, Brian Stafford and Bernard Flynn notched 11 points for the winners who went on to enjoy a golden spell under Sean Boylan.

The Ulster champions were hampered by a hamstring injury to Dermot McNicholl in training. A major doubt before the game, McNicholl hobbled his way around Croke Park on a heavily strapped leg. He was replaced before the end after battling gamely with Mick Lyons.

McGilligan's fielding at midfield was a facet of Derry's path back into the game, with Gerry McEntee managing to break enough ball to keep Meath ticking over.

Colm O'Rourke opened the scoring in the first attack, as Meath pushed into a 0-8 to 0-4 interval lead. Tony Scullion, Joe Irwin and McGilligan put in decent shifts in an opening half that saw the Oaks presented with a half chance for goal.

McNicholl went through but his shot was easily dealt with by goalkeeper Mickey McQuillan. It left Derry with the regret of what a fully fit McNicholl could've conjured from the opportunity.

With Derry's attack struggling to break down Meath's defence, it was a long way back with Boylan's men easing into the final.

★★★★★

interested in football. George Murphy had taken charge of a minor team around that time and had a brainwave to move me outfield.

I was full of running and he took me back to mark Joe Beattie against Magherafelt. He was a big Maghera star at that time and I did a pretty good job on him. I think people started to look up and think that I was a bit of a prospect.

My next run out with Derry was in the under-21 team of 1984. We played Down and I remember Jim McGuigan, God be good to him, coming over to me afterwards to tell me that I had a great game. We were well beaten that day, but I played well so the football was starting to come out in me.

Even for Dungiven at that time, I wasn't really that interested. They came looking for me one Sunday for a reserve match when they were short of numbers. I was down hutting corn in the field when they came and, that was me again, I was hooked into it. From starting in the reserve team, then I was into the senior panel.

The next year I was on the senior team and scored the winning goal when we beat Magherafelt in the 1983 county final. A high ball came into the square, I rose and fisted it into the net. That was the first championship Dungiven won in 32 years, and I have another four medals to go along with it.

I was playing hurling with Derry around that time and can remember Mickey Moran was in charge of the footballers. They were going to Kerry for the opening of a pitch in Ballylongford, a few weeks before Kerry played Galway in the All-Ireland semi-final. Myself and Tony Scullion were down that weekend and we were the newcomers on the block, along with the likes of Colm McGuigan, Gabriel Bradley and Joe Irwin, these boys who were coming to the end of their careers.

It was an eye-opener for us that weekend, to be playing against Kerry was unreal. They had boys like Eoin 'Bomber' Liston and that was my first time in the Derry panel. At that time, Derry football was a hot potato. I remember us playing Down in the McKenna Cup one Sunday in Drumsurn. We didn't have the numbers. I went to training and there were only eight or 10 people at it. Derry football was in the doldrums.

My first time playing in the championship for Derry was in 1986, against Tyrone in Omagh, and I remember Jim McKeever telling me before I went on the field to get warmed up. I told him I was ready to go, and his words to me were… 'Pull up your socks and tuck in your jersey'. I went on and within a few minutes, we turned the game and were winning, but Noel McGinn scored a super goal to win it for Tyrone.

DERRY DIDN'T HAVE a settled set-up and managers seemed to come and go every year. There were even a few barren years after winning Ulster in 1987, when we won nothing and things were poor. It all changed in the early 90s and that's when things started to improve on the way to winning an All-Ireland.

We beat Down in The Marshes to get the '87 championship run off the ground. Straight after that match, I drove to Altnagelvin Hospital to visit my mother, Mary. She died shortly after that. She would've followed me to all the matches, but never saw me getting my All Star, All-Ireland or anything like that.

Down are always a great scalp, but there was no hullabaloo about beating them. We played Cavan in the semi-final and it went to a replay. Cavan were a good team at that time too, they had some class footballers. In the first game, we were lucky to get a replay. Stephen King had put in a big display the first day and I was tasked with marking him the second day. In the second game, Paul Kealey came on as a sub and scored the winning goal

We beat Armagh in a tight final and they had a man sent off, but after winning Ulster there wasn't that much buzz going into that All-Ireland semi-final with Meath. There was a lot of talk about it, but it's not like now where you have everywhere decked out in colours.

We saw it as an open draw, any of the teams could've gone through and it was whoever was the hungriest team. The fact it wasn't Dublin and it was Meath, the feeling was we had a chance because they were first-timers too.

Then, when you saw the Meath team, they were a pretty good side too. I didn't know an awful lot about them, but I had met a few from the International Rules trip to Australia the previous year. There was a bit of a discontent over Mick Lyons, because I got the full-back position with Ireland. Before we flew out to Australia, I was playing at full-forward in all the trial matches. They'd kick it in and I would be breaking it and laying it off to the smaller boys. That tactic was working well.

When we got to Oz, there was a trial match and, so as to not show the Aussies our full hand, Kevin Heffernan shuffled the whole team about. I was put to full-back... and Jack O'Shea was put to corner-back.

I was marking a guy, Smith, who was a big star at the time for the Aussies. He gave me the runaround for a while, then I got to grips with him. He fell, got hurt and had to be carried off with broken ribs. There was a full-scale row.

By the time it came to the Thursday night before the first official match, we were in the meeting and I was named at full-back. I stayed behind to talk to Heffo and to tell him I'd never played full-back before, saying that I was afraid I'd let the whole thing down.

'I know you won't let me down!' he replied. And that was it. I have a lot to be grateful to Heffo for, he had the confidence in me.

Mick Lyons spat the dummy out, because he had a bit of an injury, but I'll never forget him down in the hotel lobby one night doing press-ups and sit-ups. He wanted Heffernan to see him and know he had recovered to full fitness again… but he never got back into the full-back position again.

That was a sore point, and that was the first time I ran into those Meath boys.

PLAYING MEATH IN Croke Park that year was a big, big deal for us. You were lucky to get to Croke Park to watch a match never mind anything else. There were no cars about. It was massive and you only dreamt of these things.

I remember being up at my grannies to watch big games on the telly. They had no electricity in the country, but they had an engine for power. For the All-Ireland finals, all the neighbours would be over and the engine wasn't put on until 30 seconds before the game was to start… and it was turned off as soon as it was over, but you were glued to it.

You'd have heard Michael O'Hehir commentating on games over the radio. Then you see it for yourself on the TV, but when you are down there playing in the games yourself, it is some step up.

Dermot McNicholl injured his hamstring on the week of that All-Ireland semi-final with Meath and it was the toss of a coin whether he'd start or not. He was injury prone with the big thighs. He was a phenomenon; he was a freak with legs on him like tree trunks, and he could run like a bullet. The rest of the team was a bit down and I would say it swayed the management to play McNicholl, so the fact he was able to play was great. However, it didn't last and he had to come off. Perhaps it would've been better for him to come on as a sub, but it's easy looking back now.

It was my first game in Croke Park, but I wasn't really that nervous. Everybody has their own way of dealing with things. On the Derry team of the 90s, some players were bouncing off walls, some were doing sit-ups and press-ups, and some were beating each other. I just liked to sit in the corner with my eyes closed… and relax. I don't get too het-up about a game.

The best way of getting rid of nerves is to get into the game quick and get in the first slap or get a good slap… the nerves are gone and you are in the game. The longer it goes on, the harder it is to get into the game. That day against Meath, I remember hitting Martin O'Connell a real humdinger and every bone in my body shook. I don't know how he felt, but he did about six somersaults and I thought he was dead. He was a wiry boy. He was down for a few minutes, then got up, gave himself a shake and hit the free.

I didn't think too much of how I was playing but I felt I was getting into the game and was pretty sharp. I was farming every day, running after sheep, so I was active and working hard as a joiner. When you are out training with a team, you got honed a bit more and you were sharper. As it went into the 90s, I was getting progressively faster.

Joe Brolly, over 10 or 15 yards would be fast, but after that they're gone. Over 100 metres, nobody would touch me. Tony Scullion would've been close… a couple of them were close, but they couldn't beat me. It was the same in the 80s and it stood to me.

Meath were four points up at half-time, but we were still in the game and we had chances. We knew we could win that game, but it was Meath who made the final. I was named as Man of the Match that night on the television, but it never really crossed my mind during the game. I knew I was doing alright because I was winning ball, was moving well and causing bother. I was putting a big shift in with tackles and blocks.

I remember being down in the dumps about it after. Whenever we went for food after the game in Dublin, word came out that I had got Man of the Match from the losing team and it was unheard of. The fact that I got an All Star out of it was an even bigger shock.

If you look from 1993, Derry had never been back in a final, so you have to make hay when the sun shines. That was our year to do something and we were on a level playing field with Meath. Cork and Galway were on the other side, so it was there for the taking, but we didn't believe in ourselves.

We weren't used to winning and you can only get belief from winning, and if you look at the present Derry team, they have cockiness because they've knocked on the door for the last two years. The arrogance is starting to come in Derry football and they are doing well at underage. Back then, we won minor titles, but never won Ulster senior titles which is a big thing.

LEAVING CROKE PARK in 1987, after that defeat to Meath, I was drowning my sorrows on the bus. I was sick and depressed and ate no dinner. I think I must've slept nearly the whole way. I was gutted.

The boys were enjoying themselves, but I was a deep thinker and wondering why we couldn't rise ourselves? If every man had given one more percent, as the saying goes, that's 15 percent. Then it's the difference in getting the ball or getting a block in… then it is the difference in winning and losing. I never, ever, thought we'd be back again.

I remember going down to Dublin in 1993 to the All-Stars. We were late and stuck in the traffic. A Dublin taxi man shouted across at me 'Congratulations'… and that I was a cert to get an All Star. When I was going into the hotel, different ones were telling me I had got it but in '87 I didn't know at all, not until my name was called out. I was surprised. Even though I had played a bit of decent football, I was on the losing semi-final team, it was unheard of.

When my name was called out, it was mad. Myself and Scullion were there, the two of us got All Stars… and we played together for the first time that day against Kerry in Ballylongford. Tony Scullion was told he was too small at minor level. With me, when changes were being made, they put on every Tom, Dick and Harry before me on the minor team.

But, then, if you didn't go to Maghera school and have the name for being an early riser, you didn't get a look in. If you go to one of these colleges, it doesn't matter if you can kick back doors or not. That's why that Meath game was significant for me. I was only starting to play on the Derry team in 1985, then in '86 I had one championship match against Tyrone and it was over.

I was lucky enough to get to Australia off the back of that without really being known. Then in '87, we got to the All-Ireland semi-final and people were asking who the big ginger boy was. It was the game that brought me to the attention of everybody, that this boy can play a bit of football. To me, it was the game that brought me to the forefront of people's minds.

There were people down south who didn't know who I was, but then in '93... even that taxi man in the traffic recognised me from being midfield on that successful Derry team.

In 1987, there were a crowd of boys coming to the end of their careers and there was a transformation after that. A lot of younger boys came in... the Downeys, the McGurks... and Tohill came back from Australia. Everything seemed to fall into place and there was a nice blend of players, young and old. There were boys like myself and Scullion, who were hungry for success, thinking we'd never get back to Croke Park... and there we were again in 1993.

25

OF THE
GREATEST
IN ACTION

★★★★★

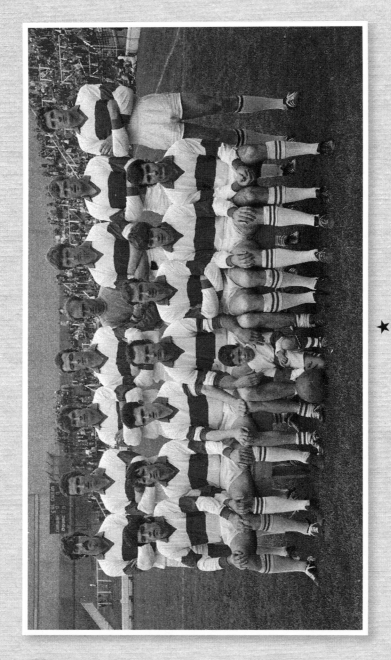

Mickey Niblock, Gerry O'Loughlin and the Derry team which lost to Kerry in the 1970 All-Ireland semi-final

Fifty years after their
victory in the All-Ireland
club final, Laurence
Diamond and his
Bellaghy teammates
finally got their hands
on the precious trophy in
Croke Park

Mickey Lynch
(left) in flying
form for Derry
in the '70s

★
Anthony McGurk (top) and Brendan Kelly both share the 1976 Ulster final victory over Cavan as the game of their life

Gerry McElhinney races through the Down defence

After starring in college in 1983, Dermot McNicholl was the 'boy wonder' who manned up for Ireland against the Aussies in the International Rules series in 1987

★

*Brian McGilligan
claims the ball in
typical forceful
manner against
Tyrone in 1997*

★

*The indomitable figure
of Tony Scullion*

Plunkett Murphy and
his brother, Andy who
managed Dungiven to
championship glory
in 1991

Having his father
as manager was
a pressure Gary
Coleman had to live
with, and when he
moved back into
defence he took
up that challenge
with gusto

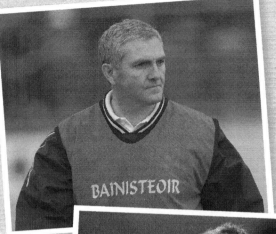

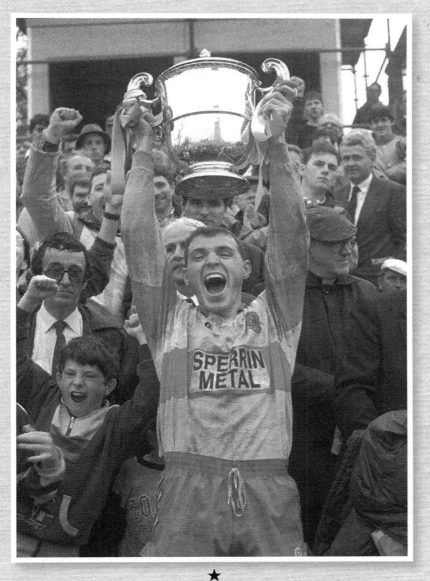

★

Henry Downey lifts the Anglo-Celt Cup after claiming the
Ulster title in 1993... next stop Dublin!

★

Enda Gormley celebrates on the steps of the Hogan Stand with Eamonn Coleman and Tony Scullion after defeating Cork in the 1993 All-Ireland final

★

The shy boy, Enda Muldoon, who often wondered if he'd be out of his depth at county level, takes his place amongst the 2004 All Stars selection

★
*Kieran McKeever
in action against
Armagh in the
2000 Ulster final*

★
*Sean Marty
Lockhart claims
the ball in defence
against Monaghan
in the 2007 Ulster
Championship*

Paul McFlynn breaks through the St Gall's defence in the 2003 Ulster Championship

*Paddy Bradley and Kevin McCloy, friends and teammates, and
winners of All Star awards with Derry in 2007*

★

Paddy Bradley leads Glenullin into battle against Bellaghy

★

Kevin McGuckin dominates against Armagh in the 2011 championship

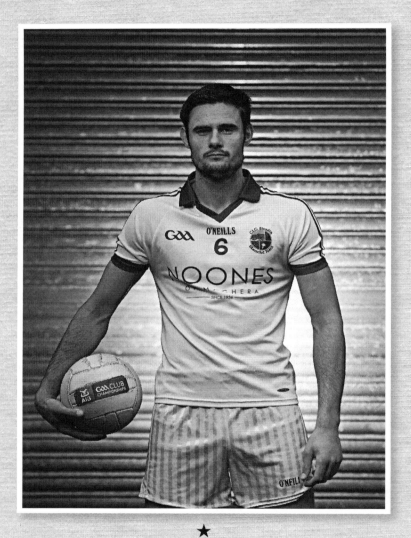

★

Chrissy McKaigue, whether lining out for Slaughtneil (above) or Derry, was made to measure in stopping every marquee forward in the country

TONY SCULLION

IRELAND 3-9-7 (52) ★ AUSTRALIA 0-7-10 (31)
International Rules Series – Second Test
Bruce Stadium, Canberra
NOVEMBER 10, 1990

★ **IRELAND:** P Comer; **T Scullion**, S O' Brien, N Roche (6); A Mulholland, P O'Byrne, M Gavigan; B O'Malley, J Grimley (16); V Daly (4), J O'Shea, P Curran; B Flynn (3), J Stynes (9), K O'Brien (13). Interchange: E Heery, T Carr, J McCartan (1), M Fagan, B Sex.

★ **AUSTRALIA:** M Campbell; S Wright, D Frawley (1), R Smith (4); J Blakey, B Stephens (3), M Hanna (8); P Couch, T Daniher; T McGuinness (1), S Loewe (2), G Brown (5); N Bruns, P Salmon, M Mitchell. Interchange: B Allison, S Malaxos (1), J Gastev, P Dean (3), G O'Donnell (3).

> ❝

DERMOT MCNICHOLL WAS only a lump of a lad when he played for Ireland in 1984, and Kevin Heffernan brought in Brian McGilligan for the trip to Australia in '86.

It was 1987, when I was called up. Ulster had played Australia in a warm-up game and I was playing for Ulster on possibly the worst day a game was ever played. It was in Omagh and it was one of those days when it didn't take time to rain. It was absolutely terrible and I can remember there were loads of children there from schools… they all got soaked.

God rest both Eugene McGee and Sean McCague, they gave me the call after we were beaten by Meath in the 1987 All-Ireland semi-final. McGilligan and McNicholl were on that panel too.

THE ACTION

★★★★★

TONY SCULLION HAD the game of his life as Ireland clinched the 1990 International Rules series with a second victory ahead of a Third Test that meant very little, only pride.

John Grimley hit 16 points in all and was a handful for the Aussies, but it was the defensive line of Scullion, Stephen O'Brien and Noel Roche who stood tall.

Indeed, Roche and Scullion played every minute of all three games in the series, with a shoulder injury forcing O'Brien off at half-time in the Second Test.

Jack O'Shea, voted as player of the tournament, dropped back to lend a hand for a more accurate Irish side, who had all the answers on the night. The strength of the home side was in their sling-down tackle, something they had in their own game, but Ireland boxed clever.

Eugene McGee and Sean McCague's charges used a kicking game and getting the ball away before contact, giving them the platform for victory.

Armagh's John Grimley, named at midfield but operating at full-forward, had the ball in the Aussie net after just three minutes, but Ireland trailed 11-9 at the end of the first quarter.

It was the second quarter where Ireland did all the damage, hitting 30 points in 20 minutes to put them on course for victory, with further goals from Grimley and Jim Stynes.

★★★★★

That's when I got my first experience of the International Rules and playing for Ireland.

Liam Hinphey, who has also sadly passed, God rest him, was the Derry hurling manager at the time and was very friendly with Eugene; they were in the same year in UCD.

In the International Rules, there were five interchange players and the rest of the panel didn't tog out. I wasn't in the 20 for the first two games, and Derry were playing a hurling match down the country before the next test.

Liam got in touch with Eugene to see would I be allowed to leave the camp in Dublin to play the hurling game, and I was. Eugene allowed me to go and I re-joined the Ireland camp for the third game.

I was selected as an interchange, coming in 10 or 15 minutes into the game and stayed on for the rest of it.

It was a brilliant experience. It was very like gaelic football but we wouldn't carry the ball too much because the Australians were absolutely superb at the tackle. They were able to lock you, as it was in their game, whereas in our sport the game is all about shadowing and nipping the ball.

We had to move the ball on quickly; that was preached to us and you soon knew you had to.

I can remember when the final whistle sounded and we had lost by a couple of points.

Eugene McGee was a man of little words. He looked at me, shook my hand and said, 'Well done, we can all make mistakes Tony!' I think I knew what he was trying to say, and that I had done myself justice. I think he realised I suited the game and played well when I came on. He was half-apologising to me for not putting me in for the other games, which he had no call to.

WHEN I HEARD those men were involved again in 1990, I said to myself that it was up to me to make the push to get on the team, as the opportunity might never come around again. As it turned out, I played every game. Back then, there were very few men who weren't interchanged in and out of a game. That year, myself and Noel Roche were the only outfield players who played the whole series, every minute of it. I was enjoying the games, it was just a great experience.

Before we left for Australia, there was plenty of preparation to get through. The

Ulster players, we would've trained at St Macartan's College in Monaghan during the week and Sean McCague was the man who took us. Everyone would've been out on the Wednesday night at four sessions in the four different provinces, but we were doing the same runs.

It was very tough, you'd be running around a field and there was no sign of a ball with Sean roaring you on. You trained hard because we needed to get miles on the clock, because we were going to be playing against professionals out there. Some county teams had been knocked out early, and everybody had to get up to the same level.

The whole squad met up at the weekend in Tullamore and it was all games with the ball, whereas in the middle of the week it was running.

Back then, times were tough in the north with the Troubles. It was 1990 and I got an awful scare going across the Aughnacloy border… four or five of us coming from a county hurling match one day, and how we were treated.

After that, I was a bit apprehensive going across the border at that checkpoint in the dark on my own. My wife, Siobhan, we weren't married at the time, but she was in the car with me when I headed to Monaghan for the training.

I was happier that she was there with me in the car when we were crossing the border at 11 o'clock at night. I'd have parked the car away from the field and she was in the car when we were training. Back in those days, we went across to the Four Seasons for food after training.

Sean asked me one night if I had somebody in my car? When I told him it was my girlfriend, he brought her in and said she deserved the food the same as the rest of us. That was the type of the man he was.

The final trial game was down in Tullamore and everything was on the line. I just wanted to get on that plane. I knew I was going rightly in training and I just wanted to give it everything. I desperately wanted to play for Ireland. I had got a wee taste of it in 1987 and I wanted it so much.

You start off and you want to get on the Ballinascreen under-14 team and if you have any aspirations of wanting to be the best you can be, you want to go up the ranks to get on the Ballinascreen senior team. Then, you push for the county… then your province, and then your country. That's the way I went out to training all the time; I trained to be the best I could be.

I never got a Derry minor trial and never thought I would get the opportunity to play for Derry seniors. It was under-21 before I wore a Derry jersey for the first time. We played Armagh in the championship in Bellaghy; I'll always remember that. We went on to the All-Ireland final and lost to Mayo, but that was me started with the county.

When I did, I wanted more and played for Ulster when we won six Railway Cups in-a-row. I captained them and never missed a second of the games in the six years.

Jesus Christ, playing for your *country*... playing for your country. It's the only opportunity we have. There is no gaelic football World Cup and this was the nearest we'd get to it. When the chance arose, I was going to give everything to try and make that, and I got there.

I am not sure how the call came that I'd made the travelling squad, maybe I got a letter. In the lead-up to it, it was all very new. Before that, I was on the plane when we toured the US with the 1987 All Star team, but this was different. Australia was that bit further and it took us nearly a day and half to get there.

There was so much to get organised, even simple things like going to the dentist. Somebody told us if there was a weakness in a tooth on the long plane journey, it would be found. I went to my dentist, Pauline Taylor, and we often look back and joke about it all.

Looking back, it was unbelievable and for that to happen to me... even before Derry were successful, it was great. Did I even think Derry would win the Sam Maguire?

Myself and Stephen O'Brien, who I played against in the '93 final, we became great buddies. There might've been three or four destinations, when we were out in Australia, and the management always had us changing our roommate.

I was with Noel Roche from Clare for the first one, and then I was rooming with O'Brien. We got on so well that in the third hotel, we swapped so we'd be together. When we won the Second Test, the third one didn't matter ... and we had great craic.

You were on the field with Eoin 'The Bomber' Liston and Jack O'Shea... legends of the game. The Bomber was my childhood hero and we have stayed good friends ever since.

THE WERE ABOUT 18,000 at the First Test in Melbourne. I remember standing looking at the Tricolour… listening to Amhrán na bhFiann and having an Ireland jersey on. It was just unreal, I couldn't explain it.

The Irish people out there, they nearly become more Irish when they are away from home and the atmosphere with them was great.

The first game was a tight one, but we won it. Then the management said it was up to us if we wanted to have a good week before we went home… to go out and win the Second Test, because the last one wouldn't matter.

Jaysus, we put some effort into that second one. For the last Test, we didn't hardly train at all, maybe for one day and they beat us by a ween of points, but sure it didn't matter. We already had the series won.

When we were out there, we prepared well. We'd have been training before the sun got up in the morning, and again in the evening when it went down because of the heat.

I remember Bob O'Malley had to wear a long-sleeved jersey in the Second Test because he lay too long out in the sun. We were all advised to be careful and I would've burned to cinders, so I lay up in the room in the cool.

There was very little downtime until the last week. It was all about the preparations and looking after yourself if you'd any injuries.

After the First Test, I got a bang and hurt my ankle. There was a big reception for both teams after the game, but I didn't get out for it. I was up in the bedroom with my leg in ice, with the physio treating me… and the dinner was taken up to me.

That was me getting ready for the second game and they were worried about me, but I declared myself fit by getting to training after missing the first day. I could've very easily missed that second game.

We were expecting a backlash from the Aussies. I was interviewed before the second game and I said we were expecting it to be very physical and if you watch it back, I was involved in a couple of heavy challenges.

It was more catch and kick with us, because we wanted to avoid the tackle. The Australians were very physical and had big men all over the pitch.

It was the second quarter with the breeze, that we pulled away. John Grimley scored another goal, a six-pointer. We were good at scoring goals, something they weren't used to in their game.

The Aussies were getting behinds instead of three pointers, whereas we were accurate in our shooting. They had as much possession as us, but we held them out well at the back.

They didn't have the elusiveness of a Peter Canavan in their game, someone who is going to go past you. They wouldn't have taken us on because they knew we could pull them down It was a different game. Australia were better than us at playing the ball through the hands; we weren't great at it because we were afraid of being caught with their tackle so we kicked the ball more.

Then, as the series went on, they started to kick it and, in that sort of kicking game, you can read that situation more when you are a defender. I would rather see the ball coming in earlier than through the hands.

I CAN STILL remember how much I really enjoyed that Second Test. We were under the cosh at times in the game but we were good at shutting them down. We did really well in the full-back line and stopped them getting in for a goal, or even a chance of one. It was a game where you just felt that you always seemed to be in the right place.

It is a team game, but you want to leave an imprint and I felt I left my imprint in those three games. Jack O'Shea was named as player of the series and I know I was in the equation for that too. A few of the Ireland players were chatting with me afterwards and told me I could've got it just as handy.

When you hear that from people across the country, it means a lot. When Eugene McGee and Sean McCague put their arms around your shoulder and tell you that, 'You are a good man' it means a lot too. Then it was time to party… and it was just bloody well brilliant. There was myself, Keith Barr, Paul Curran, Stephen O'Brien and the Bomber. The five us would've been down for breakfast… and then away down the town. You'd come back in the evening for a shave and a wash before the dinner… and away we went again.

Bomber was a great singer and he could sing any song. I remember him asking me, 'Scully, what d'ya want me to sing?' I'd always get him to sing *The Town I Loved So Well* and he belted out every word of it. They were great times. We weren't going mad, but we had a few pints and it was great craic.

The management told us it was job done and away you go. I met the McGoverns from Ballinascreen out there. You'd have met people after the matches and partied with them.

What made the whole thing was winning. I am a bad loser myself… not to an opponent, because I'd always reach out and shake his hand, but it wouldn't have sat well with me if we were beat. But to win the first two games was ideal.

Those boys are friends for life, and we would be in contact back and forward. Bomber was up at a do in 'Screen club and I've met him in Dublin for games and we'd be ringing each other for tickets.

IT WAS A great experience to play for Ireland, and I never thought of what would happen after, with Derry winning the All-Ireland and three National League titles. The International Rules was a different type of game; it was pressure. It helped me when I came back to play for Derry in the big games.

I was there in 1987 and played in all those games in '90. It certainly helped me, it gives you great confidence to stand along with Jack O'Shea and Bomber, it makes you feel very special. Where I came from, I didn't think it would happen to me, to hold myself in that company.

I was back again in the management set-up and got the opportunity with Paul Earley in 2013 to go back to Australia. I also managed the under-17 team two or three times when we hosted Australia.

,,

PLUNKETT MURPHY

DUNGIVEN 2-10 ★ LAVEY 0-11
Derry SFC Quarter-Final
Watty Graham Park, Glen
AUGUST 10, 1991

★ **DUNGIVEN:** T Tracey; M Bradley, D Heavern, E Kelly; K McKeever, B McGonigle, N Mullan; B Kealey (0-1), J Brolly; F Dillon (0-1), B McGilligan (0-1), S Heavern; G McGonigle (1-4), **P Murphy (0-3)**, R Tracey (1-0). **Sub:** G Murphy for Mullan.

★ **LAVEY:** B Regan; P McGurk, A Scullion, B Scullion; J McGurk (0-4), H Downey, Ciaran McGurk; D O'Boyle, J Shivers (0-1); F Rafferty (0-1), B McCormick (0-3), O Collins; D Mulholland (0-1), S Downey, Colm McGurk (0-1). **Subs:** D Doherty for O'Boyle, F Convery for S Downey.

66

THE FIRST TIME I started to play for Dungiven seniors was in 1978 and I can remember it well. It was a reserve match over in Ballinderry, and I was in at corner-back.

That was the first time I played football really. My father died that year and I had never played much before that. Andy, my older brother, was heavily involved, so he got me started to play. I didn't really have any interest before.

He was more into managing than playing, and was a father figure and 11 years older. Myself and Andy, we would've been the closest in our house to each other. I worked to him when I left school and we would've had a very good relationship with the football.

My house now, it was the home house at the time and I can remember Liam

THE ACTION

★★★★★

LAVEY CAME INTO this game as All-Ireland champions, having beaten Dungiven by two points in the 1990 Derry semi-final as their journey grew legs.

When Raymond Tracey's early cross was lost by Lavey goalkeeper Brendan Regan for the game's first goal, Dungiven got the perfect start to match the hunger they brought to the game.

Brian McGilligan was stationed at centre-forward on Lavey hub, Henry Downey, who had to mix plugging gaps with keeping tabs on McGilligan, with Joe Brolly joining Brian Kealey at midfield.

Derry's 1987 Ulster winning skipper, Plunkett Murphy, revelled in the new role his brother and manager, Andy, found for him as a target man, feeding newcomer Geoffrey McGonigle.

Points from Johnny McGurk and Don Mulholland kept Lavey in touch, with Tracey's goal the difference at the break, 1-5 to 0-5.

Injury forced Seamus Downey out of the game, with Damien O'Boyle also replaced at midfield for Lavey after Brolly's movement pulled him all over the place. Brian Kealey took control of the middle third, with Johnny McGurk eventually sent there before he was later tracked by Shane Heavern.

Barry McGonigle held Brian McCormick scoreless from play with Don Mulholland taking just a point off Eugene Kelly who impressed at corner-back. The hammer blow came with nine minutes remaining. First, Plunkett Murphy played McGonigle in for a point but when he picked up a Dillon pass to hit the game's second goal, Dungiven were seven points clear.

★★★★★

Harry (McCloskey) coming here trying to get me to play minor football, but I went down the fields and hid on him. I was 20 when I first really played and, the following year, I was a regular at midfield for Dungiven. I played there for the county too and was there for years.

We were always in the shakeup for the county title after winning it in 1983, '84, and '87. We could've won three in a row. In 1985, we played Glenullin over in Ballerin. A defender gave away a silly free, they levelled it and beat us in the replay before going on to win the championship.

In 1982, it was Ballinderry we played in the final and we should've won that the first day. We were winning by a point and the game was almost over. Pat McGuckin kicked the long frees for them at that time. A free came in and the ball went through a defender's hands for a '45' and Pat then pointed it to equalise the game. I was back in the square and remember saying to the defender to let it go. If he did, there would've been no '45' and we'd have held on. The game was over. It was rough and it escalated the second day when it went to extra-time and they won by two points.

That build-up, in our opinion, is what made us. That was the start of us as a team because we became men. Somebody had to stand up to Ballinderry, and we did and we still get good respect for that. That game was the making of us, the fighting and what went on, it bonded us well and we had a good manager in Andy, who would've been heavy into the bonding process.

One year, later on, we played Lavey at Slaughtneil in the championship on a Wednesday night. We were all working men and I can remember Andy calling at the job at lunchtime to take us for a feed, so we wouldn't be eating much in the evening before our match. He took us to a hotel for a carvery. We ate a good feed then and that was us set up for playing. A lot of that came from Andy, through work, and it made us close.

In 1983, that was the first time we had won the championship in over 30 years and that was the building block for what followed. We had a meeting on the Friday night before the drawn '82 final with Ballinderry. Terence McMacken was training us at the time. When he spoke, Terence said how he felt we had trained hard, were in good enough shape and well prepared for the game.

Andy came in to talk and his first words were, 'On Sunday, we're going to meet fire with fire'… and that was what we did. I can remember when we got suspended after the '82 final row. There was a great camaraderie among us. A lot of boys wouldn't have got involved, but if one of us got hit, we all piled in.

We were going to Timoney's in Draperstown to meet the county board for a hearing about it. We thought the Ballinderry boys would be there for a row, but when we went into a bar near Timoney's that night, they all bought us drink and that was the finish of it. The final was declared void, but it was later awarded to Ballinderry on appeal.

The first time we met them in the championship after 1982, it was over at Ballinascreen. It was a tight match and I was playing full-forward. There wasn't much in it until we scored 2-3 coming up to half-time; that was coming from Eunan O'Kane and Ryan Murphy, who were excellent players for us. The game was over. We were 10 points up at half-time and it was easy from then on. Standing up to them in 1982 stood to us… it made us as a championship team.

OUR RIVALRY WITH Lavey, it developed through football and hurling with most of us playing both codes. I think it came more from the hurling, that rivalry. There was always a bit of bad blood in the hurling and it came through to the football, basically the same two teams playing against the same people all the time.

We were very close to them in 1990 in the semi-final. They scored the last two points to win the game on their way to the All-Ireland the following March. Andy was back in as manager around that time. He was the oldest boy in the house and mad into the football. Our house was mad about it. Even before I was playing, it was debated in this house every day and Andy was the inspiration for it all.

He had a great way of bringing boys together and nearly all the Dungiven team at that time would've worked to him. Even all the younger boys, they would've got summer jobs with him. We all worked together as well as playing together and we hurled on the same team, that all added to the bonding.

My move to full-forward, that was a plot of Andy's. I was 33 and I suppose I wasn't getting any younger. He had come to me the year before with the idea. I had good hands on me, I was a good fielder of the ball and I wasn't selfish. He was telling me there was boys like Geoffrey McGonigle, Eunan O'Kane and Ryan Murphy coming through at that time. They were lethal scorers, but they weren't ball-winners and he told me my job was to win the ball and give it those young boys.

That's what happened in that game when we played Ballinderry and scored 2-3 before half-time… the ball came in, and Eunan O'Kane and Ryan Murphy scored it between them. I gave them the ball and they stuck it in the net.

We beat Castledawson in the '91 championship first round at Glen and there was no real talk about that game. We nearly discarded it, as our sights were set on Lavey. They really were. Lavey were the team we needed to beat and we knew we were going to meet them somewhere, if we were going to get a run in the championship. The rivalry was always there, even if they weren't All-Ireland champions. Lavey were arrogant of themselves and, like against Ballinderry, we were going out to stand up to them. They would be trying to belittle you and they were very talkative off the ball. We didn't like that; it wasn't our style and I think it helped us getting into them.

Andy built it up as a bigger match than the rest because of what happened the year before, that was the game we wanted to win and it was the game everybody was really focused in on. He always believed… and that was his motto. The buzz and the build-up to that game was massive. You could see it on the day with the crowd… they were All-Ireland champions and it was a major fixture.

Our training for that Lavey match was seriously intense. I can remember boys crying off because it was getting too hard and our man (Andy) wouldn't be giving any sympathy. We played a lot of backs and forwards at the time. Our team was very hard and it was very tough. It was really intense coming up to that Lavey game. In defence, you had Kieran McKeever, Shane and Damian Heavern. Shane went on to win Man of the Match in the final that year, and Damian was full-back… he was tough and very fast.

In the game itself, Geoffrey and Raymond Tracey scored goals that made the difference in the end.

There was another move Andy made. From watching Lavey's play in another game, he identified Henry Downey as the man who made them tick from centre-back so he put Brian McGilligan to centre half-forward to impose himself. As the game went on, we were getting the scores and were matching them. As the game headed for the finish, you were just hoping it would be over because it was a big deal beating them.

There was a fear we wouldn't see it out, or just maybe fold a bit near the end. There was a fear they would keep coming at us and I remember there was a fierce effort from everybody in tackling. It was intense, and all hands to the pump to see it out. The feeling after the game, it was unreal. A lot of people, including Dungiven people, couldn't believe we beat them because Lavey were a good side and had some run in the All-Ireland.

Other than ourselves in the team, there was very little expectation of winning but that came from Andy believing and preaching that to us at training. It came from his belief. Looking back on it, it was probably a better time to meet them. We thought it would've been later in the championship, when they had built up a head of steam.

While I scored three points, I contributed a good bit to the other boys. I can remember the report in *The Irish News* the next day... it was on the front page. **'The old and the new'** was the headline... and a photo of me and Geoffrey. I was 33 and he was about 17.

Raymond Tracey played corner-forward, but he came out around the field and was more of a runner. It was me and Geoffrey up there, we were playing on the two Scullions – Anthony and Brian. When I had played midfield in other years, I was up against James Shivers. Then it was Damien O'Boyle and Fergal Rafferty. With McGilligan pushed up on Downey, our midfield was Brian Kealey and Barry McGonigle.

In 1991, it was probably the peak of that Dungiven team, with the boys who were there from the early 80s to the younger boys coming in. We won every trophy in Derry that year... the O'Hagan Cup, the Bishops Cup, the Kerlin Cup, the league and championship. I don't think there were many teams to do that... five trophies, we won everything. It was a great year all round because we weren't always playing our full team in some of those competitions.

We thought we might've met Lavey later on in the championship, but the draw paired us off in the quarter-finals. It had us focused on this game right away and that's why we nearly slipped up against Magherafelt in the semi-final, because of the euphoria of beating Lavey. It was like a county final and we forgot we hadn't it won yet, and we nearly slipped up down at Swatragh in the semi-final. If we had, the big win over Lavey would've been all for nothing.

If we had played against Magherafelt the way we did against Lavey, we'd have won it easy. It was nearly a two-horse race at that time between us and Lavey. We were a point down near the end and I got the last two scores to win it. They were two long-range points and maybe it was God that guided them, but they went over the bar.

The last one to win it… I kicked it very high and it was close to the post. I was sure the umpire was giving it as a wide, but he gave the point and the referee was hesitant about it. It was iffy… and I was iffy about it myself, but it was given.

We beat Newbridge in the final, but it was one of my poorer games. I had very good games against Lavey and Magherafelt in the semi-final, but that was the hard work because we won the final easily, we won by 10 points.

WE WERE UNFORTUNATE, in another way, when we beat Lavey in 1991. Winning the Derry championship was the main goal and we didn't set our sights on Ulster, and were beaten by Killybegs at Ballinascreen in the first round. We shouldn't have lost but we didn't play in the second-half and when we did, it was too late as we were too far behind.

With the team we had, we put too much emphasis on winning the county championship and we didn't look at the big picture enough until the 1997 team. The team we had at that time, in the early 90s, if we had really put our mind to it, we could've gone on and won Ulster but we were content enough with a county championship and never really looked beyond that.

I remember in 1983 and '84, we were unfortunate in the draw. It was the reigning Ulster champions St Gall's and Burren both years. They had won Ulster and were looking at the bigger picture, but we weren't looking at the bigger picture enough over that period. We prepared well enough for it but it wasn't really our goal.

Looking back on our team, it was the camaraderie and the closeness of the team that made us so successful. We wouldn't have been bullied by anybody, and that made us a good championship team. I saw teams in our club that were better football teams, but they didn't have the same championship desire or the closeness to win a championship like we had.

The 1991 season was the peak of it, but it came from '82 when we stood up for ourselves and earned the respect.

99

GARY COLEMAN

DERRY 1-10 ★ TYRONE 1-8
NFL Final
Croke Park, Dublin
MAY 3, 1992

★ **DERRY:** D McCusker; K McKeever, D Quinn, T Scullion; H Downey, C Rafferty, **G Coleman**; B McGilligan, D Heaney (0-1); A Tohill (1-5), D McNicholl, G McGill (0-1); J Brolly (0-1), F McCusker (0-1) E Gormley (0-1). **Subs:** S Downey for McNicholl, J McGurk for Rafferty, D Bateson for McGill.

★ **TYRONE:** F McConnell; S Meyler, C Lawn, P Donnelly; F Devlin, E Kilpatrick, N Donnelly; C Corr (0-1), P Donaghy; A Cush (0-1), E McCaffrey (0-3), B Gormley; M McGleenan (0-1), D O'Hagan, P Canavan (1-2). **Sub:** P Devlin for Meyler.

❝

MEATH BEAT US in the 1990 All-Ireland minor semi-final and five of us moved up to the senior panel. At that time, there were four games before Christmas, so that was my first introduction to senior football. There was myself, Declan Bateson, Dermot Heaney, Eamonn Burns and Karl Diamond who came into the senior panel at the same time.

Daddy had come on board as senior manager and while I had been captain of the minor team, I was now the manager's son and I thought I had to prove myself.

Maghera had won two Hogan Cups at that time and I remember playing three years of Ulster Minor League football. With not having a full team until the Hogan Cup was over, I never won a game in three years in the league. I think we drew two games in that time.

THE ACTION

★★★★★

DERRY CAME WITH a late rally to stun Tyrone and take home the silver from a landmark afternoon in Croke Park. Anthony Tohill's goal in the closing stages had a stroke of fortune attached with his strike from a '45' slipping through the hands of Tyrone midfielder Plunkett Donaghy on the goal-line.

Tohill and Dermot Heaney added points to seal Derry's win, and it was Heaney's early goal that set the Oaks on their way to victory when the teams crossed paths two weeks later in the Ulster Championship.

Gary Coleman played a vital role in keeping Adrian Cush scoreless from play after Cush had taken Tommy Carr for five points in Tyrone's semi-final win over Dublin. A Ciaran Corr point helped the Red Hands on their way to a 0-7 to 0-5 lead. Derry hit back with points from Joe Brolly and Enda Gormley. Eamonn McCaffrey and Mattie McGleenan made a goal for Peter Canavan that separated the teams as the game headed towards a finale.

With four minutes to go, Brian McGilligan lofted a high ball into the Tyrone defence. Declan Bateson snapped up the break but was denied a goal by the frame of goalkeeper Finbarr McConnell.

The resulting '45' from Tohill went all the way to the net and Derry pushed on for a victory that laid the early foundations for taking Sam home 16 months later.

★★★★★

We played Fermanagh in the first round of the minor championship in 1989 and they were fancied to beat us and win Ulster, but we came through that day in Irvinestown. We were very poor in the semi-final against Cavan and looked to be going out of it until Eunan O'Kane came on and scored 2-2. After that, we built momentum and were unstoppable all the way to the All-Ireland.

My aim growing up was to play for Derry and my first memory was going to the 1985 Ulster senior final when Derry were beaten by a good Monaghan team. Growing up I was a mad Kerry fan. They won the All-Ireland in 1984… I was big into Mikey Sheehy, he was my favourite player.

Monaghan played Kerry in the '85 All-Ireland semi-final and the replay was on the same day Derry were beaten by Cork in the under-21 final. Daddy was the under-21 manager and I remember him chasing the referee around Croke Park… and the guards chasing daddy. He claims he was only going in to ask him a question. Those were the days when northern teams didn't get much in the south… and they were robbed that day.

My first year of minor was in 1988, when we played Down in the first round of Ulster on a very wet day in Ballinascreen. The full-forward line was myself, Dermot Heaney and Eamonn Burns and I was only a month off turning 16. It was a young team but I always remember daddy telling me I was slipping around like a Lough Neagh eel with a pair of mouldies.

The following year, we played Antrim in a friendly over in Glen. We started with the boys who were on the panel the year before, and bringing on the others at half-time to have a look at them. Our centre-back John O'Connor, from Drumsurn, went off injured late on. Daddy was up watching the game and told John Joe Kearney, our manager, to throw me in at No 6 because he always thought I was a defender. After that, I stayed at 6 for the rest of the season.

I had played all my football at underage in Magherafelt at centre half-forward or midfield. We won an under-16 All-Ireland with St Pius and even though I was centre half-forward, daddy would tell the boys I was a back. I enjoyed playing in the forwards, I was there for a good bit of my career at it… but I am not saying I would've made a county career as a forward. You never know.

FR SEAN HEGARTY took the Derry senior job in 1989 and he brought daddy in along with him with the view of stepping away after one year, and daddy would take over as manager.

Daddy had been in England working and I remember chatting to a man at daddy's wake who was on the plane home out of London. He told the man he was coming home for Christmas and was taking the Derry job. After the man told him he was crazy, daddy said he'd bring Sam home within three years.

Fr Hegarty had called me into the panel for a month or two for a bit of training the year before, while I was still a minor, but daddy didn't want me to be there. He felt I wasn't ready for it, but at 17 you just want to play football and if you get the call-up you are going to want to play. It is men against boys at that stage.

I did feel the pressure of being in the senior squad as the manager's son and that's why the 1992 league final performance is so significant… and my turning point.

In my first league game, at the end of 1990, we played Cavan in Breffni Park. Ronan Carolan was the star for Cavan. He was playing at midfield and in the last 15 minutes I was brought on to mark him for my debut. I think I did fairly well on him and we won the match. I was just on to mark him tightly and not really play as a midfielder. I started the following week alongside Brian McGilligan in a draw with Mayo at Ballinascreen.

My midfield days ended two weeks later when we lost to Kildare in Newbridge. I was taken off and had a shocker. The last game before Christmas was against Antrim in Drumsurn and they beat us. Hugh Murphy was the Antrim manager and the headline in the paper that day was that the fathers dropped their sons… as Hugh's son, Chris was playing for Antrim.

It was daddy's first game as manager after being confirmed in the days before. I was a late inclusion at wing half-forward when someone got injured, but when I missed a goal chance, he whipped me straight off. We turned it around after Christmas. We beat Tyrone at Celtic Park, and we took another win in Longford. We had a big meeting after that and it was the time the Lavey boys had won their All-Ireland and were coming on board. The Lavey and Dungiven boys didn't like each other from rivalry at club level, but it was cemented after that.

For me, I was just on and off the team in 1991. We beat Tyrone in Omagh in the Ulster Championship preliminary round and I was an unused sub. When we played Monaghan, I had hurt my hamstring and only came on as a sub in both Down semi-final games that year in the Athletic Grounds. It wasn't until the following season that I became established in the team. Most of the other boys that came through from my minor age were already getting on, but I suppose daddy felt under pressure that I had to play even better.

He would admit it himself, he was really, *really* harsh on me. The other players will admit he was harder on me than the rest. He also knew what I needed. For some people, an arm around the shoulder works, but he knew I needed an eating for me to perform. In his second stint as manager, when I was one of the more senior players, it was totally different because I was established. We always talked football but not about our team. He wouldn't tell you that you played well, but he'd tell you your mistakes.

If we were coming home from a match and he said, 'You done rightly today!' then I knew I'd played well.

I LET HIM down in 1991. I was playing for Newry Town in the Irish League at the time and we were allowed to play up until Christmas… and then you have to make the decision to pick soccer or Derry. You were also not allowed to play on the Saturday before a National League game.

We played Kildare in Ballinascreen late in the year on a really bad day and I had played soccer the day before. It was the days before the internet and I suppose I thought nobody would find out. Daddy lifted me at the house and we went to Draperstown to get food on the way to the game. He never said a word in the car, so I thought I had got away way with playing soccer the day before.

At our meeting in the Corner House, he tore strips off me in front of everybody. Players at the time said they wouldn't have taken it and walked out. Even though he did tear strips off me, he wouldn't hold grudges. I was dropped and not allowed to tog out that day. There was driving wind and rain, and we always would play with the wind if we won the toss to build up a lead. He made me stand up on the bank behind the goals with a spare ball for every kickout and go to get the other one that had gone over the fence, so Kildare couldn't waste time.

I came in at half-time drenched to the skin… he said, 'Kildare can get their own ball-boys now'. That was it over. I was back at training on the Tuesday and it was as if my soccer game had never happened. It was up to me to learn from it, so I quit the soccer and never did it again.

Daddy and the management set out at the start of 1991-92 season that we had to go to Croke Park and win the National League. Derry had been going down for years and getting thumped. We needed to go to Croke Park to win, just to prove to ourselves we could live with, as he would say, 'the big boys' in the south.

We played Meath and beat them in the semi-final at Croke Park. I remember being on Tommy Dowd that day and he was a big strong man. I wasn't that long out of minors and his power was tough on me. That was the turning point for me because we sat up in the front row of the Hogan Stand to watch the second semi-final, Tyrone against Dublin.

They had Peter Canavan and Adrian Cush, who had won the under-21 All-Ireland. Adrian was a brilliant footballer and he scored five points from play off Tommy Carr that day. I was sitting there watching him. He was right half-forward and I knew I would be marking him in two weeks' time in the final.

The whole build-up to the game was talk centred around the Canavan and Cush show. Peter Canavan and Kieran McKeever had super battles and played well on each other. The narrative was that I might as well not turn up because Adrian was going to destroy me, because he was a fabulous footballer, but daddy said I was the man for Cush and that I would take him.

I knew this was my moment. You'd have always heard people saying I was only on because I was the manager's son. I had a blinder on Cush that day. He hit one point from a free in the whole game and I got on Team of the Week at the time… which was a big thing.

Adrian is a really lovely fella and I have got to know him since, but he was trying to talk to me during the game. I would keep staring ahead because I didn't want to engage. I didn't want to get friendly with him because, on that day, it was either him or me.

My battle with Adrian was bigger than that actual game, it was about convincing people I was good enough. I didn't respond to him, not that he was saying anything bad. I didn't reply with anything at all… I tried to do that with all my opponents

I remember myself and my wife, Paula, were out on holidays in Santa Ponsa. It was about five years after the game, and Adrian and his wife came walking down the street and we got talking.

He's a really good fella and I have a lot of time for him, but in those days when I was marking him, you just had to look at one thing. It was him or me and he was up on a pedestal from the semi-final and I wasn't. Tyrone… they had Peter Canavan, Mattie McGleenan and Adrian Cush. They were the three main men, so I thought about the help it would be if I would take Cush. I knew from marking him that he was left footed and he was playing at right half-forward, so at some stage he was always going to have to cut in. I encouraged him all the time to come in because he was coming into traffic.

I got up the next day and bought the paper. I was in great form. We had won the league and beat our great rivals, but when I opened up the paper I was like a beaten bear. It gave me a good report, but Cush said he was fouled every time he got the ball. For me, I prided myself on good tackling and that gave me the determination two weeks later when we met them again in the championship.

Adrian scored a point from a free in both games and he was totally out of it. He wasn't involved… I had totally dominated him. You knew by daddy's body language after the league final that he felt I had done the job. He knew the first day that I had him again in two weeks' time.

Mattie McGleenan gave Tony Scullion a very hard time in that league final, and there is that famous story of daddy bringing out a newspaper article in the dressing-room before the championship re-match in Celtic Park. The paper was all about Mattie's total admiration for Tony, but daddy didn't let him see it. He told him the article was about Mattie, saying, 'I finished Scullion' and 'Scullion's done'. It was stuck up on the door and it was one to those things you don't really look at, but Tony just crumbled it up and threw it down.

Tony destroyed Mattie that day and after the game somebody picked up the article. I saw what was really written, but daddy knew how to get into Tony's head.

There would've been some boys who would come in with the big hit as a defender. I was lighter at the time and it was about making myself big, getting my hands out and having pride in not letting your man contribute to the game. Even if you are not in the game! You couldn't be in the game if he is on the ball, but you are tackling like blazes to not let him past you. I did pride myself on that.

Maybe that's why daddy said I was a defender. In those days, it was a battle. We always talked about if we could win 12 of the 14 outfield positions, then we'd win the match. Now it is completely different but, back then, you had to win your one-on-one battle before you'd even think of helping the team.

THAT LEAGUE FINAL win over Tyrone was also very important for us as a team. People felt we'd beat them on a smaller pitch like Celtic Park, but they'd beat us in Croke Park. That was the narrative before the game and Tyrone probably did play better than us on the day.

When Anthony got that lucky goal, the game was still level at 1-8 each. We kicked the next two points, so we upped it and they were shellshocked. We won the championship game 1-10 to 1-7 two weeks later, but it was a three-point hammering.

Those matches changed our mentality. When the management were telling us we were good enough to win an All-Ireland it was like what Jim McGuinness told Donegal. They were good enough to win an All-Ireland, but until you started winning things then it's only words. It was the same with us.

After that league final, we were able to say we went to Croke Park and we beat Meath... that Tyrone beat Dublin, and we beat Tyrone... so we were good enough to go there and win. It does give you belief. Before that, maybe there was a doubt about whether we were good enough. If Tyrone had beaten us in the league final, an All-Ireland might not have followed with that doubt in the mind of going to Croke Park and not winning.

It would've been another day where Derry got beat in Croke Park, so it was psychological and we needed that.

We beat All-Ireland champions Down at Casement in the Ulster semi-final. It was a huge result and performance, we probably took our eye off Donegal in the final, thinking we had the hard work done because they came through the easy side of the draw, whereas we had beaten Tyrone, Down and Monaghan.

John Cunningham got sent off that day for Donegal and I was the spare man in that Ulster final. It was probably a bit of inexperience on my part. The next year, it was Johnny McGurk who was the spare man in any games if a man was sent off and the bit of extra experience helped the team, with the management figuring those things out.

We realised that we let Donegal away in 1992. Going into '93, we realised the three best teams in Ireland were in the one province... Donegal, Down and Derry. We then took out Down and I believe that wet day in the Ulster final saved Donegal from taking a hammering. We were so ready for that game and the weather kept it close.

When Donegal went on and won the All-Ireland the year before, we were sick. Down had won it the year before that again… they had broken ground. We were so determined in '93. We were good enough, there was only really Donegal, Down, Dublin and, to a lesser extent, Cork, but they had the four years where they won two All-Irelands and lost two. They were coming towards the tail end of their span as a team.

We were in the top four or five, but there was no backdoor in those days.

I had no fear in the All-Ireland final, even when John O'Driscoll scored Cork's second goal to put them one up. We had come back from five points down, and had beaten Dublin who were a better team.

Training was going that well, that you never think you are going to get beaten. We didn't feel that, but I still point it all back to 1992 and getting that run in the league… getting to the final, winning it… and getting that belief.

Belief is a everything.

DAMIAN CASSIDY

DERRY 0-15 ★ DOWN 0-12
Ulster SFC Semi-Final
Casement Park
JUNE 28, 1992

★ **DERRY:** D McCusker; K McKeever, D Quinn, T Scullion; J McGurk, H Downey, G Coleman (0-1); B McGilligan, D Heaney (0-1); A Tohill (0-3), D McNicholl, **D Cassidy (0-3)**; E Gormley (0-6), S Downey, D Bateson (0-1).

★ **DOWN:** N Collins; B McKernan, C Deegan, P Higgins; J Kelly, P O'Rourke, DJ Kane; L Austin, E Burns; R Carr (0-3), G Blaney, G Mason (0-6); M Linden (0-1), P Withnell, J McCartan (0-1). **Subs:** C Mason (0-1) for Higgins, A Rogers for Austin.

66

I HAD BEEN injured for most of the National League with a torn hamstring. We were trying to push at the back end of 1991. It wasn't until the semi-final of the National League that I was able to train fully without any set-backs. I got on the panel for the final… and I had to get myself back into the team at that stage.

After beating Tyrone in the championship preliminary round, we played Monaghan in Castleblaney. We were cruising in the first-half before the wheels came off spectacularly in the second-half. I came on in that game and did reasonably well, so I was selected for the replay in Celtic Park.

I had a really close relationship with Eamonn Coleman, stretching back to the minors and it went on over the years, I was very fortunate that he approached me to get involved in the management with him in 2000.

Everybody was lined up that day in Celtic Park and ready to go out the door,

THE ACTION

★★★★★

THIS WAS A novel pairing of the reigning All-Ireland and National League champions locking horns in front of 33,000 fans, and under the baking Belfast sun.

It took a late Ross Carr free and a replay for Down to sink Derry at the same stage 12 months earlier. After winning the league, it was Derry's time to deliver.

Kieran McKeever, Danny Quinn and Tony Scullion did a number on Down's potent inside trio. Brian McGilligan and Dermot Heaney were a formidable Oakleaf midfield partnership.

And Declan Bateson, Damian Cassidy, Enda Gormley and the galloping Anthony Tohill were all on target as Derry went in 0-8 to 0-5 ahead at half-time.

The atmosphere was electric in front of a bumper crowd, wedged into every space, as the teams threw everything at the game. Down had another spell in the game, but when Peter Withnell was sent off on a second booking, Derry were able to absorb what was thrown at them.

The hurt of losing the previous year only inspired Derry further, with a Gormley free and a curling Heaney effort opening up a gap. When Seamus Downey's over the shoulder fist pass found an in-form Cassidy in space, he curled over the insurance point.

Aside from booking an Ulster final place, the victory was a big statement, given Down's stature as All-Ireland champions with a team who would be back to reclaim Sam two years later.

★★★★★

after all the blood and thunder of the team talk. Eamonn stepped in front of the team and stopped them going out the door. He turned and he aimed at me saying, 'Cassidy, I am telling you, today's your last chance… you need to play!'… and he sent us out onto the pitch.

The one thing about Eamonn, he knew everybody's mind and he knew how everybody ticked. There were other players he never did that with and it would've been a totally different tact, but that was such an unusual thing to do with everyone just wanting to get out the door.

I played well in the game and that took us into Casement Park against Down, who were All-Ireland champions… and they had to be beaten. Eamonn would've talked about the three teams in Ulster… Down, Tyrone and Donegal, but particularly Down. They were the aristocrats of Ulster football; they had four senior All-Irelands and were on a pedestal at that stage.

Apart from trying to get to an Ulster final, we all knew we had to beat a team who were All-Ireland champions, but we had the confidence gained from winning the National League.

This was the game. We are talking about Mickey Linden and James McCartan and Greg Blaney. I can remember Eamonn specifically really getting at Henry Downey to do a job on Greg. I can remember him saying to Kieran McKeever in terms of doing a job on McCartan.

There was a focused level of aggression that was in his whole demeanour towards that game, that was not the same as it was towards Donegal. It was the intensity of playing Down and what Down meant to Eamonn in his own playing career, as well as losing the replay the previous season in the Athletic Grounds.

He also knew they were a county that when they got a head of steam up – like when they were All-Ireland champions – they brought a level of football confidence that other counties could never get to.

We knew Casement Park was going to have a big crowd because we knew we now had a following. I remember the boys carrying the banner 'Derry on Tour' to all the games. Coming up into Casement Park that day, the crowds were getting bigger and bigger as you were coming up towards the pitch. You were starting to realise that playing the All-Ireland Champions brought a level of razzmatazz we hadn't experienced before.

It was just a cauldron, even the way Casement was designed. It was an amphitheatre. You had the stand; the seating was curved going around the back of the roadside goals and there was a steep grass bank on the opposite side of the stand, and that day it was all full of people. A wall of faces.

You were coming out into an absolute cauldron to play the All-Ireland champions and they are bringing the self-belief that they are there to defend their title. In their heads, they are going for two in-a-row. For us, we had won the league but we had been pipped the year before by Down. We had to get over the line. There are only so many times you can go to the well and fool yourself that you are good enough.

There has to be a sense of realism in it. If we lost that game, then where were we back to? We were back to being beaten by Down again. That would have been three times we had played them in 12 months... and we wouldn't have beaten them. Eamonn could sell the dream so many times but, eventually, the players have to start living it themselves.

We had a group that was focused, that was used to success coming through at underage with Derry minors and under-21s and colleges football. You also had the boys involved in the Sigerson football. You did have a group of players who had that level of ambition and proved they had the ability to play at that level, but you have to still go and do it.

Maybe if I hadn't been involved in football management after my playing career, I would've had a different perspective on it. But knowing the path that teams take, there are games that come along that have to be won to get to the summit. Even though you have to win it in terms of the pathway, the psychological pathway is more important because that's where the real deep-seated belief comes from.

Looking back, I can feel the intensity Eamonn had going into that game and the specific people he drilled that into, to get a performance out of them.

Blaney, who I really admired as a player, hadn't a massively influential game and Kieran did a powerful job on McCartan. Danny Quinn did a pretty good job on Peter Withnell, who eventually got sent off. An awful lot of players won their individual battles that day. There is that iconic photograph of Anthony kicking the ball in full flight. That captures perfectly the athleticism of Anthony. He was simply a magnificent footballer.

The game itself, it was just an absolute mental war. I can remember big

McGilligan just battering people. It was incredible. I have no qualms in saying, he was the strongest man I have ever played football with or been involved with in football via management. Without a doubt. The other thing that was under-sold about Brian… he was very quick.

The first time I realised what McGilligan was like was in a National League game against Offaly. McGilligan went down to pick the ball up and that's when you are really vulnerable. One of the Connors, who had played in the Offaly team that had won the All-Ireland in the famous game where they prevented five in-a-row for Kerry, came into him… as he was down in the position of picking the ball up. He'd have been 6'2" and about 14 or 15 stone, and he drove in and hit McGilligan. The rest of us would've been scattered, but the guy just bounced off him.

My father-in-law had a saying that it takes all sorts of players to make a good team. You can't have too many of the same type of player and the role Brian played was critical to that team. Coleman knew how to challenge him. He used big Stevie Mulvenna to get the best out of Brian. Coleman knew how to work him.

I hit the final point of the game. The ball had been played down the sideline on the stand side and Seamus Downey came out and won it about 35 yards from goal. Between collecting it and moving it on at the same time, he had executed a 25-yard pass with his left hand, not his strong right hand, so I just had to take my time and set the shot.

There was never a stage in the game I thought we weren't going to win. The energy of the team never went down, the morale never dropped at any point. You had two really good football teams and it was a battle of wills to see who would give in first.

I haven't watched that many games but that was one I did watch back about 15 years ago; it was just the experience of what Casement Park was like.

That Down team beat us in 1991 in the replay and had to be put away. As it turned out, they subsequently proved how good a team they were. They came back and won another All-Ireland in '94, after we crushed them in '93 on The Marshes. That core of Down players were an outstanding group of players.

It really accentuates how critical that victory was on the path we went on to win an All-Ireland. There was an absolute intensity that carried through that entire game. For me, it never dropped. There was never a lull in what was coming off the crowd and onto that field with the nature of how that game transpired and developed. It was like the All-Ireland semi-final in '93. Maybe there was a bit of a lull in the first-half, but in the second-half the crowd were just bubbling all the time.

That '92 Ulster final was still a winnable game. Anthony going off was massive in it, he broke a bone in his foot 20 minutes into the game and went off at half-time. I remember meeting different people in the weeks and months after the game. They were saying we threw that Ulster final away… we threw an All-Ireland away.

We didn't. We weren't playing a game that was good enough to win an All-Ireland, even though we had the footballers to win an All-Ireland at that stage.

WE LOST TO Donegal in the 1993 league quarter-final and we had a meeting at the next training session in Ballymaguigan after it. There were hard conversations and people were given a chance to air their opinions. I got the feeling it was universally agreed that we needed to retain the ball more and create more of a running game, supporting the player off the shoulder as well as a kicking game. Prior to that, we let the ball out much more and there was less support play off the shoulder.

If you look at the type of football played by Derry in 1993, compared to '92, you can see a marked difference with that running support play off the shoulder. I think if we hadn't have done that, regardless of how good a group of players we had… I just don't think we'd have got over the line.

The players had that absolute belief that we are going to win it. There was seven or eight weeks until the championship. I can remember Eamonn leading that meeting and Mickey Moran being heavily involved in that discussion of drawing out people's options. Following that, the emphasis was there about what we were going to do going forward.

You still can't get away from the belief the players had, to get to the point where I am meeting Sean Donaghy, RIP, in Kilrea in January of 1993. I remember telling him, 'Sean, we're going to win the All-Ireland this year'. I was absolutely convinced.

That's the evolution and that's where Mickey deserves credit in that regard. Eamonn brought him in after '91 as a coach, and that's where his strength lay at that particular time. He was coaching us to keep the ball more, and create that running off the shoulder game and what was needed in the coaching environment to make that happen.

For me, there are certain games on our journey. Beating Tyrone in 1991 was one part of that. We probably needed the draw and to be beat by Down to make us realise we were not a million miles away.

The following year, 1992, that win over Down, in terms of a pathway, was absolutely critical As I said previously, people will turn around and say we threw away an All-Ireland, but it was 1994 or '95 where the other All-Ireland was lost… it wasn't lost in '92.

We weren't playing the right football to win an All-Ireland and that meeting was a change of emphasis and the coaching that went along with it.

In the 1993 Ulster final, we are going to that well once again and it's a similar situation to Down in '92, in that Donegal were now All-Ireland champions and they had to be beaten. Donegal had beaten us in the Ulster semi-finals in 1989 and '90, in the '92 Ulster final. Then there was the league quarter-final of '93, and there had been a friendly in Banagher where it turned out nasty at the end with a bit of clipping done. There are not that many times you are involved in your career when you just know you are not going to be beat. That Ulster final, for me, was one of those games. It was like the final of the All-Ireland with Cork. It just never entered your head, the thought of getting beat.

It was all feeding into this intensity Eamonn brought and, of course, then as individuals that you would bring yourself.

IT WAS ONLY really in the warm-up, when we were sprinting and turning that we realised what that surface was like. We had seen the minor game, but it wasn't until we hit the pitch that we realised the full extent of what the surface was like.

But it was the same for everybody. You have still got to play football, to get your first touch, give the passes at the right time… track their runners.

One of the greatest experiences of being a county footballer, apart from playing, is going to the games and as you gradually get closer to the venue, the crowd starts to build and the bus gets quieter. You are just a bus with a team in it, and you are mates. The closer you get to the venue… the quietness starts to come in, the focus just descends on the team.

Coming up Clones Hill with the crowd breaking for the Garda escort, it creates that unique experience you'll never have in your life again unless you are involved in management. I remember coming into Clones and the rain was thumping down. I couldn't believe how far the cars were parked out the road and how far we had to go to get to the field.

For us, we felt we were genuine All-Ireland winners and I have no qualms about saying that. We were totally convinced in our heads. We just had to get over this game to get to where we needed to go to. So, that's why that game, to me, in terms of the group, the focus and the build-up was so similar to 1992 against Down.

I can just recall about 10 or 15 minutes into the second-half when I could feel the team starting to stamp itself on the game. We were starting to win too many battles throughout the field and we were never going to lose that game, outside of a flukey goal in the rain.

You could feel the gap between the teams coming in the game. There were a few massive moments, with Tony's block, and Brian getting the hand in to cut out a goal chance. You would expect a team of Donegal's absolute quality as All-Ireland champions to make that drive. They will point to players not playing but that's marginal because, ultimately, what it comes down to at that stage is that massive self-belief.

During that period in Ulster, there were very few teams able to back up their success the following year. The demands that were placed on players, the intensity and the quality that existed in Ulster at that stage… it was unparalleled and hasn't been seen since.

Tyrone and Armagh were close in the early noughties but they were still short another team. We are talking about three teams who were in their pomp, had credentials and proved it. It was a unique time in Ulster football… and for Derry, a very special time.

ANTHONY TOHILL

DERRY 3-11 ★ DOWN 0-9
Ulster SFC Quarter-Final
Páirc Esler, Newry
MAY 30, 1993

★ **DERRY:** D McCusker; J McGurk, D Quinn, T Scullion; K Diamond, H Downey, G Coleman; **A Tohill (0-4)**, B McGilligan; R Ferris (1-0), D Barton (0-1), D Cassidy (0-3); D McNicholl, D Heaney (1-0), E Gormley (0-2). **Subs:** F McCusker for Scullion, E Burns (1-1) for McNicholl.

★ **DOWN:** N Collins; M Magill, C Deegan, P Higgins; J Kelly, B Burns, DJ Kane; B Breen, E Burns; R Carr (0-5), G Blaney, G Mason (0-2); M Linden (0-1), P Withnell (0-1), J McCartan. **Subs:** G Colgan for B Burns, G Deegan for E Burns.

66

THE DECISION TO come home was taken for me. I was released from Melbourne Football Club halfway through the 1991 season. I had gone out, like a few before me, and played in the under-19 competition for a year.

At that time, each Australian club had under-19, reserve and senior teams, so they had a lot of players on their list. In 1991, the under-19 competition was done away with and lists were basically cut in half, so clubs started looking at players who were surplus to requirements.

In my case, I was costing them a lot of money. I had just started a five-year double degree course in Civil Engineering and Business Administration. It was costing A$16,000 a year to educate me, on top of my digs, my bit of subsistence, match payments… flights back and forth home.

THE ACTION

★★★★★

THE HURT OF leaving Clones empty handed in 1992 spilled over the rain-drenched Newry sod as Derry laid down the marker for their magical summer.

And Anthony Tohill put on a tour de force. He plucked both throw-ins and missed little in between.

Down and Donegal had edged out Derry on their way to winning Sam in the previous two years, but there was no denying them on this occasion.

Johnny McGurk launched a ball from corner-back into the midfield minefield. Tohill was head and shoulders above everyone with a text-book high catch, before drilling a long ball to Damian Cassidy, who sliced over the first score of the game.

By the 16th minute, Cassidy added a second and Damian Barton picked out Dermot Heaney with a perfectly weighted pass before he slotted under Neil Collins for a 1-3 to 0-2 lead.

Derry kept their foot to the floor.

This year was going to be different.

At the other end, Damien McCusker judged his angles to perfection to save from Ross Carr.

Richard Ferris buried a second Derry goal, after Collins denied Burns in the build-up. By the time Burns volleyed a loose ball to the net for Derry's third, it was a rout which led to Pete McGrath, in his post-game interview, telling fans they were owed an apology by everyone connected to the Down team.

★★★★★

They looked at me and essentially said, 'You're costing us too much money, and you are free to go home'.

It was very loose back then; things are better now for the lads going out. It was almost taken on good old fashion trust that they'd look after my education. That was the only thing my parents were concerned about... that I would get my education.

They did that for my secondary school no problem... in a really good secondary school in Melbourne, St Kevin's. And they put me through the first semester of university.

I broke my leg six months into my first year in Australia and was out of action for the rest of the season, missing a good bit of pre-season for my second year. The injury happened playing gaelic on the QT. All the Irish lads played gaelic... Jimmy Stynes, Sean Wight, Brian Stynes. The clubs knew we were doing it and turned a blind eye to it, until I got injured.

I should have been playing in the under-19 Grand Final in the MCG in September, but missed it due to the injury so that didn't help my chances.

I worked hard and recovered, regained my fitness and was playing reserve team football. I thought I was going okay. It wasn't my idea to come home but the decision was taken for me so, once it is out of your own hands, you have no control over it.

I rang home to tell my parents and it was my father that answered, and he seldom answered the phone. I told him I was coming home and he replied, 'Good man'. After that, I spoke to my mother to see what could be done to get me into university in September.

I didn't have A-Levels, so luckily I got into university on the strength of my Australian qualifications. That was the hand I was dealt at the time and you hadn't much choice... I had to make the best of it.

I CAME HOME and within a day or two I was at Derry training. The 1991 championship was already underway. Derry had beaten Tyrone and we were playing Down in the next round. I was on the bench and came on in the second-half. I scored a point and must've done enough as I started the replay.

There wasn't a lot of time to adjust back into it, but it wasn't difficult to adapt back to gaelic. It's not like now. Australian Rules was semi-professional in 1991 and you weren't coached to within an inch of your life. I didn't get any other coaching above what any Australian was getting. We just trained... there was very little individual coaching.

It was either sink or swim, whereas now, the game is fully professional and there is so much coaching and support available.

I suppose it made it easier to adjust back. I was only there a year and a half, seven months of it out injured, so I hadn't lost my gaelic footballing ability and, of course, there was the odd gaelic game on the side.

Switching back, I didn't find it that difficult to adjust, albeit our campaign in 1991 was to be a short one. In the drawn game, Ross Carr kicked a point from what was, at best, a 50-50 chance from a dodgy free kick. We thought we were close, and when we watched them go on and win an All-Ireland we thought that maybe that could have been us. In truth, we weren't ready to win an All-Ireland. I don't feel we, as a team, were mature enough and ready to do what Down did. I don't think that true belief was in us. I think we were at a different stage of our development.

Down got on a nice roll, and there is nothing like the Down men with a bit of confidence behind them to see something through.

When we entered 1992 we felt there was every chance we could win the All-Ireland. We won the league, which was really important for us. It was the only time, in all my years playing for Derry, that any manager went out with the intention of winning the National League.

I remember, vividly, Eamonn Coleman saying we should go out and try and win it. He and the management team felt that winning a national title would give us that genuine belief that we were good enough. Back then, the National League was really important. There was no backdoor in the championship and, as the second national competition, it was held in a lot more esteem than it is now.

Winning it in '92 was huge and it gave us that belief. It was only the second time in Derry's history that a national title had been won at senior level, so we were confident that we could take the next step and go on and win the All-Ireland.

We came to Casement Park to play Down in the Ulster semi-final... Down, the All-Ireland Champions. We were smarting from what happened the year before. You know it is going to be a hell of a game and when you come out on the right side of that, then you know you are very close.

The belief was there that we could go the whole way in '92, but Donegal had other ideas. I played the first 15 minutes and I had a collision with Tony Boyle. I was trying to clear the ball and ended up connecting with his knee. I broke two bones in my foot and played on for the rest of the half, but had to come off at half-time.

We ended up losing by a point or two, and it was a sore one to take... a really sore one. We did think we were good enough to win and, to be fair to Donegal, they showed they were good enough and won the All-Ireland.

You can imagine what the mood was like in Derry at the start of 1993. Nothing but an All-Ireland was going to be good enough for us. We had the confidence, we were really, really hungry for success and determined to avenge what we thought we should have had in '92... and possibly in '91. We were so focused going into that '93 campaign.

People ask you what it was like to have won the All-Ireland and you say it was the most natural thing in the world... we expected to win it. We had put so much into it for that three-year period, on top of all of the training and success players had in their careers coming up to '93.

It was just natural for us and that sounds crazy coming from a Derry man, who had never ever won an All-Ireland ever before to say that we felt this was natural. It was what we expected and nothing less would have done us that year.

It wasn't a hope or an aspiration, we genuinely believed we were good enough. It is one thing believing and it's another thing going out and doing it, but going into Casement against the All-Ireland champions in 1992 and beating them, that was a massive, massive result for us.

That took us into an Ulster final with Donegal. They were able to approach that game with a little less fuss. They were a bit more focused and were a great team as well. They were fantastic on the day and deserved to win.

EAMONN WAS A great character. He never complicated anything, he had a really genuine way of saying things and I suppose that came from his own football career; his own life and what he had worked at.

It came from knowing how to deal with adults; how to get the best out of people and what made people tick... from knowing he can give one man a bollocking, but needed to put an arm around another. He was a players' man and a very astute man in how he managed people. He lived and breathed football, that's what Eamonn Coleman lived for.

He also had a really good football brain and the whole set-up around the team was where it needed to be. Mickey Moran was a wonderful coach, there was no one better then or since, and they were a great partnership. Two different characters that got on really well together. The backroom set-up was good, support from the county board was miles away from what it is now, but it was enough for what we needed. The county was pulling behind us and the clubs were pulling behind us, so everything was right, all the ingredients were there that you needed.

DERRY FOOTBALL AND the entire GAA community lost one of its best when Eamonn passed away in 2007. There was a lot more that he could've achieved had he still been around.

As a team, we had a good balance. You had three really, *really*, experienced senior men in Tony Scullion, Brian McGilligan and Damian Barton. You had a handful of fellas who had won an All-Ireland minor in 1983, a handful who had won an All-Ireland minor in '89 and a handful that won an All-Ireland Club in 1991. You had men who had won Sigersons during the same period, so there was a lot of success within that group.

There was also a lot of ambition, guys who wanted to win and were ruthless with other aspects of their lives, and were prepared to make the sacrifices to achieve our goal. It was a great group of players and all the ingredients were there – both on and off the pitch – so it was over to us to make sure we delivered.

The preparation for that 1993 Down game began the very first time we met after the defeat in the Ulster Final in '92. There were no doubts or second guessing about what we were there to do. Our focus was to go the whole way and not just to win our first championship game. When we were drawn against Down in Newry, things were brought into a sharper focus.

Earlier in 1993, we had lost to Donegal in the National League quarter-final and I suppose that was a wake-up call. There was a ding-dong session after that to try and straighten things out. I can remember Eamonn and Mickey had brought in a guy called Craig Mahony. He came in on the athletic side, for the fitness testing and stretching. He was a colourful guy with a different accent, flamboyant.

We never looked on him as a psychologist, and if that was his role, we were none the wiser.

You can imagine what the aftermath of that game was like, Derry had ambitions of winning the All-Ireland. Everything was going grand and along come Donegal and beat us again. It was time to get everyone in the room and take stock of where we are going and get the dressing-downs that were coming to us for how we played.

In the meeting, Craig asked a few direct questions of a few fellas, to iron out some of the difficulties and to start looking ahead to the Down game. We were going into The Marshes, having taken Down's All-Ireland title off them the previous year. You can imagine what that game meant to Down, and how up for the game their players were and how big an occasion it was going to be. Everything was on the line again, against a team that had every reason to get one back at you. Sometimes that revenge instinct that is in sportspeople can be more powerful than anything else.

We were expecting a real belter of a game against Down and we knew we had to be at our very best. Our training was first class, really intense and we were ready for it. On a personal level, when I look back on my own career, it was the first championship game I had played after getting an All Star in 1992.

I was in a different category now, where people are looking at you in a different way. Your teammates and management expected you to perform, the opposition have a tighter eye on you than they had the year before… and the supporters are expecting you to deliver more.

I certainly didn't feel it was pressure. I knew myself what I needed to do. I always went out to do the best I could for the team. Looking back, you want to get into the game early, you want to put your stamp on the game if you can. The first opportunity I had was to win the throw-in and set the tone… luckily that happened and we got on top early.

You set the tone from the first minute… the first ball, the first engagement with your opponent, but you have to keep doing that. We got a goal early; it was a great ball from Damian Barton to Dermot Heaney. That was massive as well. Momentum can shift and sometimes an early goal is the worst thing a team can get. Fellas can sit back and get a bit complacent, so the opposition usually responds when they concede an early goal.

It was one of those games where we retained that dominance throughout. I don't think there was ever a time in the game where Down were having a spell and we were in bother. I think from start to finish, we were on top. After the game Pete McGrath went out and called the Down performance a 'shambles' which were very strong words from their own manager.

I think they underperformed, but we were right at the top of our game that day and we did not allow them into the game. We were never going to lose once the pattern was established early.

You get a sense from the intensity in training leading up to game and you'll know if the team is in the right place or a bit off. Right through that '93 campaign, our training was fantastic, there was never any let-up in intensity, effort or energy.

That's where your panel comes in. There is not much made of the 14 other fellas that were on that panel. People tend to remember the starting 15 in the All-Ireland final. They didn't see how hard all 29 men trained, nor do many remember what happened throughout the campaign.

Joe Brolly and Seamus Downey weren't even togged out for that match against Down in 1993. They were standing in the stands, but they both played key roles in us winning the All-Ireland, so it just shows you how things can change.

From our perspective… other teams were looking at us thinking, *Derry, they were close in '91, but they didn't win that game. They should've won in '92, but they didn't. These guys don't have it. They can't close out tight games and they don't have it in them to win tight championship matches.*

Beating Down on their own turf, having taken their All-Ireland off them the year before, I think it made a lot of people sit up and take note that we were genuine contenders.

Up to that, I think the doubts were there with people outside the group. The Derry supporters… I am sure plenty of them had doubts. There would be a cynical few amongst them at the best of times. The belief we had inside the group was not matched by those outside the group.

I remember some aspects of the game, but as time goes on, sometimes your memory comes from what you have seen on TV, rather than through the eyes of being there. Maybe it would have been better not to watch it, so you remember it as it was.

During the lead up to that game, I was at university and it was exam time. You weren't spending every waking hour thinking of the game, wondering how you might play and who might be on you and what they are going to do to try and put you off your own game.

I was either studying or I was training, and that's what my life was like for two or three weeks before that championship match. Maybe in a way that helped. It was my second year of Civil Engineering; it was hard and we had a lot of exams. There were no modules, we had it all at the end of the year and in a way, it stopped you getting too anxious about the game.

Going in the next round, against Monaghan, you are coming off a fantastic win against Down and the expectation levels are through the roof. It took a good while to get on top of them and Joe Brolly came off the bench to kick a few nice points. We got it done, but the Monaghan game was far from convincing.

We were now in another Ulster final against Donegal... and we had the disappointment of losing the Ulster final to them the year before. There was the added spice of losing the National League quarter-final to them as well. I would say we were more ready for that game than we were for the Down game, with a couple of championship games under our belt. We were flying in training. In all my career playing for Derry, that period at the start of that '93 campaign, I never trained more.

We were training four nights a week. Our normal nights were Monday, Wednesday and Friday. Then, for a six-week block, we were going Monday, Tuesday, Wednesday and Friday which is more like teams are doing now... and that was back in '93.

It was all pitch-based. Mickey's training was superb, it was mainly football related with some running, but not a lot... it was about honing our skills and perfecting our game plan. That block of training really stood to us and when we went into that Ulster final against Donegal, we were in prime physical shape.

EVERYONE WILL REMEMBER the weather. It was low-scoring – 0-8 to 0-6 – and if it happened now there would be some complaining. It was a game that should never have taken place in those conditions... the pitch wasn't playable. For us, it was about surviving and getting across the line. That game could've easily gone the other way. There were two pivotal moments near the end. There was a block Tony Scullion made that was goal-bound. There was another when a ball was passed across the goals and Brian McGilligan got a big hand on it to intercept it. Had he not got there, it was a certain goal… a goal on a day like that would've been curtains.

We did enough to get through and that was all that mattered. It was great to win the Ulster title, but we were through to the next stage and our goal was to win the All-Ireland.

There was lots to learn from the game as well. Eamonn and the management were sorting out the personnel and the best set-up for the team. It probably wasn't a bad thing because it kept Joe Brolly under the radar. He was fantastic against Dublin in the semi-final, largely unknown, but he delivered in Croke Park.

Dublin in Croke Park, I would've said it doesn't get much bigger than that, aside of course, from winning the All-Ireland. The Dubs had lost to Donegal in the All-Ireland Final in 1992, so there is the scenario where they can't let another Ulster team beat them in Croke Park.

They had some fantastic players and it was a great game of football.

A lot of people talk about the final because it is the big game they see repeated on TV, but the semi-final was a real belter of a game. It added to the occasion that it was Dublin. We weren't fussy who we played, we had a job to beat anyone who came in front of us. It could've gone either way. When a Derry team comes to Croke Park, they don't have a massive history of success in All-Ireland semi-finals. But the belief was there from the success players enjoyed at other stages of their career. The National League behind us… beating Down in The Marshes and Donegal in Clones. We weren't going to crumble… and we saw it out.

Against Cork in the final we certainly didn't think we would be five points down early in that game. You have to gradually try and find your way back into the game. Johnny McGurk got the first point, and things started to fall into place. It's easy saying there was no way we were going to be beaten, but without the fellas standing up and doing what we did, we would've been beaten.

You can have the best laid plans in the world, but once the ball is thrown in, it's in the hands of the players on the pitch. The manager can make a couple of changes and has a chance to chat to you at half-time, but outside that… it's you and the boys around you. It's about taking your own personal responsibility to make your own contribution and I think, on that day, every Derry player stood up and made a contribution to that victory.

It was the realisation of a boyhood dream, but it was also the most natural thing in the world. We set out to win it, we needed to win it and we achieved it… so there was that feeling of relief that we had done it.

I had just turned 22, so I was one of the younger fellas. Other guys had soldiered for 10 or 12 years for Derry and finally got across the line. If you had to write it, you'd rather it came at the end of your career instead of spending 10 years trying to win another one, and failing.

I remember the final whistle and seeing my da on the pitch after the game and it was only the third time, he had seen me play live… my ma and da being there to witness that was very special. I remember going back up the road and realising this means more to so many more people than it does to me.

Some of the die-hard supporters in Derry who never would've thought they'd see Derry win an All-Ireland, they followed Derry for years, faithfully… never having ridiculed players or spoken out of turn… Derry supporters to the core.

For me, it was what we had to do and we did it. It was a case of enjoy it, but then settle the heads and let's go and try to do it again.

99

DAMIAN BARTON

★ **DERRY:** D McCusker; K McKeever, T Scullion, G Coleman; J McGurk, H Downey, F McCusker; A Tohill (0-1), B McGilligan; B McCormick, **D Barton (0-1)**, D Cassidy (0-2); S Mulvenna, D Heaney, E Gormley (0-3). **Subs:** D McNicholl (0-1) for Heaney, J Brolly for Mulvenna, K Diamond for McNicholl.

★ **DONEGAL:** G Walsh; JJ Doherty, Matt Gallagher, B McGowan; M Crossan, P Carr, M Shovlin; B Murray, Michael Gallagher; J McHugh, M McHugh (0-1), J McMullen (0-1); D Bonner (0-1), M Boyle (0-2), J Duffy (0-1). **Subs:** M McShane for Bonner, A Molloy for J McHugh, M Gavigan for Michael Gallagher.

66

THERE WERE AN awful lot of contributory factors coming into that 1993 season. The rise of Down in '91, who we would've played quite often in the Ulster Championship. We were very familiar with them... and the '92 Donegal team, who also went on to win the All-Ireland.

There was also Lavey's All-Ireland win in 1991 and if you look at their success, there was a whole acceleration of emotions that made us think, *We can do this...* and be the third Ulster team in-a-row to win Sam. There was never an occasion when there was a grain of doubt in that Derry team in 1993.

While it wasn't deemed that significant at the time, Derry beating Tyrone in the league final of '92 was another factor and this all accelerated into a belief that this year, 1993, was going to be different. We started training on the sixth

THE ACTION

★★★★★

THAT DAY IN the rain. Mention those words to any Derry fan and it will take them all the way back to July 1993.

It was a day when Derry's Cathal Scullion had his leg broken in the minor game. The newly laid pitch in Clones and a deluge of rain wasn't a good mix. Ask anyone from Donegal, and the game should never have been played. It's hard to disagree.

The collective Derry squad message was simple... Snow... Hail.... Rain... Dustbowl... it wouldn't have mattered, Derry were coming home with the Anglo Celt Cup.

Donegal hit the first two scores, but Derry got to grips with the game and two Enda Gormley points settled any nerves.

Brian McEniff's men were a point ahead at the break, but Derry came with the storming second-half Donegal brought 12 months earlier. Eamonn Coleman asked his players to go out and win their individual battles. And they did.

Tohill and McGilligan were immense. Damian Cassidy skated through the puddles to kick a second point. Damian Barton rode a shoulder charge to land an important score.

Still Donegal came clawing at the game, and it took Tony Scullion's full-length block and a McGilligan intervention to prevent Donegal getting the goal they needed to hang on to their titles.

★★★★★

of January 1993. From that day, our focus was very, very evident in everybody's mindset. Everybody, and I mean *everybody*, was so committed.

When you are part of something like that, there is an impetus. It was January, and we didn't play in the Ulster Championship until the end of May, but there was a psychological momentum. Players create the environment and you play the way you train. Mickey Moran's training was awesome and it was so enjoyable. Every night you went to training, there was something different. It was challenging, yet measured and deliberate. More significantly, you learned to trust the person beside you more than you ever did... and respect them as well.

If there was a line or a cone in training to hit, you'd go to the mark before you'd make a turn... and everybody ran to it. Nobody had to be told off for stopping short.

Whenever you are part of a squad and seeing that, I think it engrains a mutual respect. You don't have to like the people you play with, but you certainly respect the effort they make towards that common goal and cause. I do think that anything that happened in 1993 was significant from January 6.

When the championship draw was made, you didn't need to say it, you felt a palpable sense of everyone desperately wanting the Down game. We were able to focus on Down quite early. It wasn't talked about that much, but you could tell... you could tell the focus was on playing against a formidable Down squad backboned by men like Greg Blaney, DJ Kane, Barry Breen... you sensed it.

Whenever we had Down to focus on, we knew the significance of that game... especially as we were going to The Marshes. I was 30 at the time and had been about that squad since 1981. I was just out of minor and came on as a sub in the Ulster semi-final against Down. I was just in awe of Liam Austin and Monaghan's Hugo Clerkin, amongst other guys at the time. They were giants in terms of footballers and being physically imposing.

I was hanging about a long time, from Division Three and back up, and I did think on more than one occasion about retiring. I don't care who you are or how much experience you have, you want to be playing. Despite the experience and self-belief, at times you weren't sure about Eamonn Coleman and what perception he had of you. Perhaps that was one of Eamonn's strengths.

Would I have a big enough impact on the game? Had I still the legs? Because there was a lot of pace within the squad? You always felt a wee bit under pressure. I would say there were very few people who didn't feel under that pressure. Henry Downey, Kieran McKeever, Enda Gormley, big Anthony and Brian McGilligan were shoo-ins.

Eamonn had great currency in big Brian, and what he brought. Not just the brawn and the muscle, but that man's level of fitness that year was phenomenal.

There were a few changes that year. Not least Craig Mahony, who was the team psychologist. I am sure he quickly realised GAA players were mad. There were subtle changes, and you could sense the environment was different. You can't compare the 1993 mindset and approach, to the '92 Ulster final defeat to Donegal, but at least there was something tangible in the league win that you could hold on to and nurture into '93.

At that stage, Ulster football was on such a high. You knew what you were going to get with Down and with Donegal. They were the teams at the top table and there was an unspoken belief that we could get there.

I remember that year, and every player is different... but I remember that year vividly for obvious reasons. Emotionally, I was different. I used to wear the same thing to winter training every night, an old collarless shirt that you would've said was a casual one. When you were getting wet and mucky in it, you felt good in it.

Coleman said, and I did believe he was sincere, that no team was as fit as us at stages during that season and that was something that gave us great confidence. It was a universal fitness, right across the entire squad.

At that time of the year, it is wet and it's mucky. You remember Ballymaguigan and other grounds around the county. The training was tough, it was difficult and therefore enjoyable. To me, it propelled that sense of belief and add in the fact of everybody being so focused from an early stage. That built the crucial component of trust that you don't appreciate until you start playing competitive football.

I trusted everybody's fitness was good and they'd always give one hundred percent... because they didn't stop short at that line or cone in training.

I was never the fastest in the world, but I could keep going. I remember when we were doing the 200 metre runs, I used to always try to tag on with Anthony or Rooster (Fergal McCusker) because you knew they were in the faster group.

People were vying for a tow... they'd push themselves and get in with people who were a bit faster. It might have ended up a group of eight or 10, but you were never left behind and you knew if you were in that group somewhere, then you were making progress. The significance of such was that it set a template and that worked its way on through January, into February... and all the way to the end of the season.

I will never forget playing matches at training. It was quite incredible. If the game was 10 minutes each way and you thought you hadn't got into it, you'd be saying, *Play another 10 minutes Eamonn... or Play another 10 minutes Mickey...* and it was dog eat dog.

There was a whole lot of quality footballers vying to get a place. I never felt secure with Eamonn because you never knew what way he thought. He never told you where you stood, but you could easily read his expressions.

AFTER WE BEAT Down in Newry, in a strange way, the focus was then straight to Donegal. That wasn't being arrogant, because there was no arrogance in the squad, but we knew we had to beat Monaghan to get to the final, and it was squeaky bum time for a while that day in Casement.

At that time, the rivalry between Eamonn and Brian McEniff was respectful, yet intense. You have to know the personalities. What they had in common was that they were desperate competitors.

Brian was very polished in the way he came across, but when we were playing Donegal and he was on the line, you heard him and it was often colourful in another sense. He was very, very competitive and successful on many levels.

Coleman and him fused because they actually realised they had similar traits. Two desperate competitors, but two Ulster men. Having had a few conversations with Brian McEniff since, he was an Ulster Gael to the core and he wanted us to get over the line and win the All-Ireland, if Donegal couldn't.

I will never forget that day in Clones and our mindset. It spawned from the training sessions we had, with everybody having their shoulder behind the wheel and the confidence of having taken a few steps forward. The weather was not significant to me... it had no significance to any us whatsoever. I was sitting beside McGilligan for a few minutes on the bus coming into Clones from having food in a hotel in Monaghan.

The emotion was beginning to build and you could've heard a pin drop. I remember saying to myself, and I said it out loud... 'I don't give a f**k if it snows!' Because we were going to win that day and I really felt it amongst the squad, particularly in the weeks before, and on that day.

In a team environment, going into battle, you feel that sense of inner confidence in each other. You sense the anticipation and we were all feeling that on the bus. Nobody needed to say anything.

The match was never going to be called off, but we probably didn't realise how bad the pitch was. Somebody said there was water lying on it and, regrettably, Cathal Scullion had broken his leg in the minor match. We had looked at the pitch but, for me, it didn't have any significance and it was never going to be a readymade excuse. The game was going ahead.

We knew in our mindset that we were going to play that match. If there was any doubt or mindset of a cancellation, then we could've lost. We were all dialled in. It was attritional, and you know what Donegal bring to the game. With boys like Martin Shovlin, big Brian Murray and Donal Reid, it suited people like that.

We were blessed to have what turned out, and proved to be, the two best midfielders in the country. There is absolutely no doubt about that, it wouldn't have mattered what permutations other teams would put in there, you still knew you were going to win midfield.

I didn't even remember until recently that we had to change our jerseys that day into long sleeves. Matthew Gribbin, my brother-in-law, packed up the short-sleeved jersey, with Ulster final 1993 on it from the set we had for the final.

He gave it to me last Christmas, and I had forgot all about it, that I had given it to him to wear for the All-Ireland series.

On reflection, one significant thing was that none of our defenders scored that day. Anthony scored a point and the rest came from the forwards. When you jump forward to the Dublin game... Henry Downey hit two, Johnny and Gary weighed in with points. We, the half-forward line, became a defensive unit almost against Dublin and it left space in front of Joe.

Looking back to the week before that Donegal game, Henry had an awful big role to play. His exterior was always calm. He was a fantastic leader. He was always very candid, calm and confident about the squad. There was very little emotion. He didn't say very much, but when he spoke... people listened. When you felt he was cool and calm, then it translated across the rest of the team.

Henry was a massive driving force as a leader and he led by example, the way he did all through the championship.

As it got closer to Sunday, everything had been said and it was quite calm.

There was very much a momentum emotionally, as much as there was physically. Most of that game was a blur and, as a forward, you always want to score and I was happy when I got the point in the second-half.

I'm surprised I didn't pass it, like our first point in the All-Ireland final against Cork when I passed it to Johnny McGurk, and he put it over the bar. People ask me why I didn't shoot, but it's like the game now… there was an instinct to pass.

WE WERE TWO points down against Donegal early on, but it didn't matter. It was like being five points down in the All-Ireland semi-final and final. It wasn't even spoken about. It had no significance. We knew we could beat Donegal. Everybody was in a zone and the conditions had no significance. There was an overriding thought amongst the entire squad, one of trust. It was massive.

You knew McGilligan was going to get the next ball… or Tohill was going to make the next run… or Tony was going to get a hand in without fouling. There was this innate thing that none of these guys were going to get beat.

If I flip on to the 1995 Ulster defeat against Tyrone, there wasn't that depth of inner belief in it. Maybe it did have significance with Eamonn not being there, and so on, which proves the point that everything has to align. And I mean everything, but you can do a lot to align things and we did.

Everything needs to be right and the personalities on that team had an unbelievable level of maturity.

People talk about what county players are giving now. Gormley was out kicking frees after training and Ben Glancy, our doctor, was out with him with a book and taking notes. How many people back then were doing things like that to prepare? We knew that winding run of Enda's would end up in a score and he kicked the first two points that day in Clones.

Collectively, we dogged it out. They were All-Ireland champions the year before and it proved we could beat them. It was the respect we had for them as footballers, as a team and the way McEniff had them.

When we beat them, he was so magnanimous in defeat. Once they were out, and with genuine sincerity, he wanted to see another Ulster team go on and win the All-Ireland.

We had been in Croke Park in '87 and lost to that Meath team on its way up. Winning the Ulster title was massive because it opened the door of getting to Croke Park. We weren't at the level back then, but we realised we could play there. We weren't that far away but it took us six years to get back, barring the 1992 National League final which was a stepping stone in itself.

THERE WAS ANOTHER significant moment in the build-up to playing Dublin in the All-Ireland semi-final when we went down to play Meath in a challenge game.

I am not sure if Eamonn put them up to it, but Sean Boylan and Colm O'Rourke came into our dressing room after the game to have a word with us for what seemed like an eternity. Colm was standing there berating us and I think it was to give us a realisation that we were going to play the football force that was Dublin three weeks later.

We had all played against Colm, but he was borderline insulting us, saying we wouldn't stand a chance if we performed as we did that day. Colm wouldn't have minced his words and knew what winning was all about, as that Meath team did with their blood, guts and thunder…and footballing capabilities.

We were second best in most positions that day, but we weren't hammered. It was only the opening of a pitch, but it was more than that and it maybe did give us a kick in the backside. At that stage people were playing for places and we just weren't good on that day. I think the tongue lashing and dose of reality actually punctured us and took us down a bit.

It was the reality of it too. Meath couldn't beat Dublin in the Leinster semi-final and here was a team that kicked our backsides, so, on reflection, that was a very significant game for us in many ways.

If you are not one hundred percent committed in an aggressive sport, everything else is irrelevant. He probably thought we had too many nice footballers. Even to this day, I still think he insulted us and he didn't give us our place, that we were Ulster champions and had beaten the two teams who had won an All-Ireland previously, in Down and Donegal.

That day brought us down and gave us a dose of reality. It gave us the motivation that we had to be better. I think everybody took it the right way.

99

HENRY DOWNEY

DERRY O-15 ★ DUBLIN O-14
All-Ireland SFC Semi-Final
Croke Park, Dublin
AUGUST 22, 1993

★ **DERRY:** D McCusker; K McKeever, D Quinn, T Scullion; J McGurk (0-1), **H Downey (0-2)**, G Coleman (0-1); A Tohill (0-2), B McGilligan (0-1); D Heaney, D Barton, D Cassidy; J Brolly (0-1), S Downey, E Gormley (0-7). **Subs:** K Diamond for Quinn, D McNicholl for Cassidy, F McCusker for Barton.

★ **DUBLIN:** J O'Leary; C Walsh, D Deasy, P Moran; P Curran (0-1), K Barr, P O'Neill; J Sheedy, P Bealin (0-1); E Heery (0-1), D Farrell, P Gilroy (0-2); C Redmond (0-8), V Murphy, P Clarke (0-1). **Subs:** M Deegan for Deasy, M Galvin for O'Neill, J Barr for Clarke.

❝❝

LOSING THE 1992 Ulster final to Donegal was an awful setback to us at the time.

In the semi-final, we had beaten a Down team in Casement Park who were the All-Ireland champions and they'd 14 of their winning team back playing. Ulster was a minefield and to beat Down was a massive result for us. It was a huge game to win but, then, to lose in the final was hard to take because after knocking out Down, we felt we were challenging for an All-Ireland.

Before the 90s, Down were the only county really stepping up to follow their All-Ireland winning teams of the 60s. The good Derry teams in the 70s didn't get there. Tyrone were in the final in 1986, but there was no real blueprint for any other Ulster team to win an All-Ireland.

THE ACTION

★★★★★

DERRY STORMED BACK from five points in arrears at half-time to bring down the Dubs in their own backyard, and take the penultimate step towards lifting Sam Maguire.

It is a day that will live long in Derry folklore with both teams throwing everything at the game until John McGurk landed the winner. Derry raced out of the blocks to go three points ahead, before Charlie Redmond opened Dublin's account. Dublin clawed their way back into it, before pulling clear to lead 0-9 to 0-4 at the break.

It was an afternoon that saw Derry coach, Mickey Moran deliver a passionate plea to the squad. This wasn't going to be the same as the days in the 70s when Derry took hammerings at Croke Park. They answered his call in spades. Anthony Tohill and captain Henry Downey hit points to cut the lead to three, with Brian McGilligan also launching an inspirational score.

Dublin were always able to keep their noses in front as the game morphed into a shootout. It was a case of if you score, we'll score. With 10 minutes to go, Joe Brolly's rasper went over the bar to cut the gap to a point. Gormley levelled matters, before Henry Downey surged forward to kick a second point... and Derry were ahead.

Redmond's converted free tied the game before McGurk's winner.

★★★★★

It looked like the best you could do was to get out of Ulster. When Down won the All-Ireland against Meath in '91, it was obviously huge for themselves of course, but it was big for everybody else in Ulster. Beating Down that day in Casement was a massive confidence boost for Derry.

It projected Derry forward, but what a fall from grace in the Ulster final. We were poor on the day, compared to how that team evolved onwards into '93, in its makeup, its style and the way that it played. We were raw and I don't know if we would've won an All-Ireland in 1992. Maybe Donegal were a bit ahead of us… or maybe we would've done it?

We lost Tohill before half-time in that '92 Ulster final and maybe if he had not got injured, we might have sneaked out a win and got ourselves over the line. Then, when Donegal went on and won the All-Ireland, that probably consoled us a bit and it changed the whole landscape.

Now, the last two teams to have beaten us had taken Sam home… and we knew we were as good as them, so we were right in the mix. Eamonn Coleman was our manager and Mickey Moran was there too, so there was a good structure. There was reassurance all was still in place, and it was back to business again for 1993.

WE WERE ALL back playing for the clubs and then we started into the preparation for the part of the league before Christmas, so Eamonn had a full hand to pick from. We lost to Donegal in the league quarter-final, and then we had Down looming on the horizon in the championship and a trip to The Marshes.

That was a serious rivalry; we had dethroned them the previous year, we knocked them out and now we had to go into their own grounds. We had no Kieran McKeever that day due to suspension. Seamus Downey was injured, and Joe Brolly was only coming into the fold at that time. Also, Tony Scullion had gone off injured and was only on his way back from an earlier injury picked up against Louth in the league.

Those were the difficulties we had to deal with, but it was a massive win. I don't know if it was the fact that Down probably underestimated us, or they just couldn't get it going in their own ground with the pressure. I'd say they threw the kitchen sink at it to get back, but we beat them and that was massive.

That set us up for the rest of that '93 campaign. Now we were ready. As bad a setback as losing to Donegal was in the '92 final, there couldn't have been a more perfect time to win a big match since that disappointment.

I was worried about going into The Marshes in '93, but it was the coming of age of Tohill. Anthony had some game that day. He won both throw-ins and sometimes that can set the trend. We had also acquired the skills of Craig Mahony as a sports psychologist and he chipped in as we began our preparations for the championship.

There was the meeting in Ballymaguigan shortly after we lost to Donegal in the league quarter-final. Craig sat Kieran McKeever down and put it to him about not being able to play in the first championship game after getting sent off for a strike in the Donegal league quarter-final defeat. Craig stressed about the importance of discipline and how a moment like that can put you out of important games. There was an uncomfortable silence before McKeever replied, but Craig wouldn't let go of it.

He asked Kieran why he had done it… and if it was something that could be addressed? McKeever eventually looked up.

'You'll find out something Craig… after a while,' he replied. 'That's just the f**king way I'm built. So… move on.'

After beating Down and Monaghan, we went on to the Ulster final and we made no mistake against Donegal this time. I never thought we'd lose to them for a second year but I was concerned going into the Down game.

WE HAD DUBLIN in the All-Ireland semi-final, but they weren't mentioned until we had overcome Donegal. If anything, the Ulster champions were in a better position than at any time before going down to Croke Park. It was nowhere near a case of going down for the day or to make up the numbers. For us, we were going down to win.

Up until that, ourselves and Dublin missed each other in the league and we'd never even played them in a challenge match or any serious competition at all. It wasn't as if Dublin were out of the reckoning, they were there or thereabouts but we just hadn't crossed swords with them. They probably didn't know what to make of that Derry team. If they had been playing Donegal again, they could've got their match-ups from the previous year's All-Ireland final, but this was totally different for them.

For us, getting out of Ulster and getting ready for an All-Ireland, we had five weeks to prepare. It's not like now where there is a quick turnaround. There was no club football at that stage. We were training on St Patrick's Maghera school pitches a lot, we were in Ballymaguigan and had plenty of great sessions under lights in Glenullin. At one point, Coleman had to close the gates because too many people were coming to watch training such was the excitement growing across the county. It wasn't because he was worried about people spying on training or anything like that. Kick-outs hadn't got the secret codes like in the game now, so it wasn't about hiding any tactics. Eamonn was very accommodating but he knew there was a time to just get away from the crowd and be serious about it. The big problem would've been if we got caught up in the occasion and then, before you know it, time slips away and you haven't the work done.

That spell of preparation, after winning Ulster, as we got ready to face the Dubs was brilliant. It was a lot more concentrated in our sessions and training games under the lights up in Glenullin.

From a supporters' point of view, I'm not sure if the fact we were playing Dublin had any greater significance. It was football mad in the county at that time. The gap from the 70s had never been filled. We had been out of Ulster in 1987, but that was dipping the toe in it; it wasn't as strong as this. It was definitely a better squad and opportunity.

Before the All-Ireland semi-final, myself, Karl Diamond, Brian McGilligan, Anthony Tohill, Danny Quinn, Eamonn Coleman and Sperrin Metal headed down to Dublin in a mini-bus to meet the Dublin press. I think it was to get more publicity for Sperrin Metal at the time and I can remember there being a teddy bear with a Sperrin Metal logo on it.

We were in the Gresham Hotel with journalists from the various papers in Dublin. After the interviews, the photographers had us out in O'Connell Street with the teddy bear for photographs. Then we began to get a bit peeved off with it all. They were making us throw it up… and catch it for photographs.

When the photographers asked us to throw it up one last time, I just threw it at them and said, 'Throw it up yourselves and catch it… we are away'. Coleman looked at me and I just said that was enough of that… and it was time to get out of there.

WE HAD WON the National League at Croke Park but there is just something special about playing the Dubs, with the Hill being there and a packed house. Everybody wants to play against the Dubs. We hoped the momentum we had would be in our favour. Never mind Donegal having beaten them the year before, we had built our own momentum.

Coleman had picked our team up in 1990, and we climbed the leagues. We had been in two Ulster finals, and won the National League. On the way, we had beaten the last two All-Ireland champions, so we were in a good place.

We ended up five points down at half-time, but maybe us breaking from the parade before it got to Hill 16 psyched up the Dubs and their supporters. I don't really know how it happened… it wasn't planned. I turned around to say something back to Kieran McKeever behind me. As I turned around… I think he thought I was breaking. He blames me… that I said, 'Go!'… so it must have got lost in the noise and translation. The whole Derry team broke and we were booed by the Hill. Dublin kicked some great points in the first-half, but it's not as if they ran away with the game. We didn't miss much that day either.

After a good start and going three points up, we ended up five points down at half time. Inside, it was a bit numb in the dressing-room during the interval. Mickey Moran then spoke up and was making comparisons to where we had come from and how we'd get back here. He had been a player in the 70s, he had been there in All-Ireland semi-finals and had to go up the road with his tail between his legs, to try and recover from it.

'Not this team!' he told us.

He told us this would be different. He was emotional and he was angry. It was like the jump leads we needed. Back out on the pitch, I thought there was a bit more responsibility taken. I think if you look at the scorers in the second-half, the half-back line all ended up scoring. McGilligan scored… Brolly was scoring, and Gormley was scoring. It was a shoot-out.

It's not that anybody changed anything or that we made any substitutions at half-time. McGilligan's point to close the gap to three points was probably as good a motivating factor as anything else. Joe Brolly had a chance for goal that would've shot us into the lead, but his kick went over… and there was just a point in it. Enda Gormley had a free to level it, before I put us a point up.

We were in front with time nearly up at that point, but Dublin won another free under the Hill and I remember Charlie Redmond saying to me that nobody deserves to lose… that a draw would be a fair result. He composed himself, and kicked the free over to tie the game again.

Those last few moments were played in a frenzy of excitement and we managed a last gasp point to see us through, probably in one of the most memorable games in Derry's history and certainly one of the most dramatic. To win that game, and knowing you'd be in an All-Ireland final, was fantastic and the hype in the county just increased even more.

That semi-final, like the win over Down in Newry earlier in the season, was huge. Many had said over the years that the semi-final win over Dublin was a bigger game than the All-Ireland final itself, but I don't agree. The final is the *final* at the end of the day and Cork had hammered Mayo by 21 points in the other semi-final, so that sobered us up.

It is very hard to get away from the win over Dublin because it had everything, and everyone was focused on that, but Cork dismissed Mayo like they were a Division Four team. The final was the toughest game. That wasn't easy, as Cork were no poor outfit. Not by a long way. They were physically strong all over the pitch.

You knew you were in an All-Ireland final the four weeks coming up to it. The occasion got massive as it closed in, but the semi-final stood to us. Coming through a rollercoaster of an experience like that always sets you up for the next one.

ENDA GORMLEY

DERRY 1-14 ★ **CORK 2-8**
All-Ireland SFC Final
Croke Park
SEPTEMBER 19, 1993

★ **DERRY:** D McCusker; K McKeever, T Scullion, F McCusker; J McGurk (0-2), H Downey, G Coleman; A Tohill (0-3), B McGilligan (0-1); D Heaney, D Barton, D Cassidy; J Brolly (0-1), S Downey (1-0), **E Gormley (0-6)**. **Subs:** D McNicholl (0-1) for Cassidy, E Burns for S Downey.

★ **CORK:** J Kerins; B Corcoran, M O'Connor, N Cahalane; C O'Sullivan, S O'Brien, T Davis (0-1); T McCarthy, S Fahy (0-1); D Davis, J Kavanagh (1-1), B Coffey; C Corkery (0-5), J O'Driscoll (1-0), M McCarthy. **Subs:** D Culloty for T McCarthy, J Cleary for M McCarthy, C Counihan for Corkery.

> ❝

THE PENNY REALLY dropped for me when I was watching on in Croke Park as Down won the All-Ireland in 1991. Having grown up playing both with and against those boys from a fairly young age, it got you thinking…

I remember going to Derry's 1975 and '76 Ulster Championship games and All-Ireland semi-finals. At that time, you never won any games in Croke Park. That wasn't just Derry, it wasn't any of the Ulster or Connacht teams unless they happened to be playing each other.

You grew up with a mindset that the best you could do was to win Ulster. To win Ulster in 1987, I thought in the back of my head, even though you would never admit it… that was as good as it was ever going to get.

When Down were 11 points up against Meath in the '91 final, and eventually

THE ACTION

★★★★★

DERRY'S SUNDAY TO remember got off to the worst possible start.

First, Tony Davis lofted over for Cork, before Joe Kavanagh cut through the defence and hammered to the net, the first goal Damien McCusker had conceded in the championship. Cork pushed five points clear before Johnny McGurk ended Derry's rocky opening with a fine score into the Hill 16 end, under the noses of Derry fans.

Derry picked up momentum and when Damian Cassidy's drop-shot was fisted to the net by Seamus Downey, the game was on the turn. Niall Cahalane was lucky not be sent off for a box on Enda Gormley, with Tony Davis the opposite when he received his marching orders for a lunge at Dermot Heaney.

Anthony Tohill kicked a whopping point, Gormley curled over a fine shot on the run, and Joe Brolly jinked inside Brian Corcoran to score. Derry were 1-9 to 1-6 ahead at the break with Gormley hitting four points before a Cork fightback.

Don Davis assisted the first goal and it was his cross-field pass that made another for John O'Driscoll, who shot Cork back in front, 2-8 to 1-10. It would prove to be Cork's last score with Dermot McNicholl, Gormley and Man of the Match McGurk adding scores to cement Derry's place in history.

★★★★★

won by two, there was just this sudden realisation. *Was this just a once off, or could we do that?*

I remember Eamonn Coleman's speech at a meeting in Lavey before the start of the following season. He had a very clear message that we were going out to win the league, and that was our next step. He told us we were closer to an All-Ireland than you'd think. That was Eamonn. He always thought bigger than anyone else.

I remember when he was involved with us in UUJ. On the night before the 1986 Sigerson final down in Cork, we were putting in time by picking Derry teams as Eamonn always loved doing. All he ever thought of was Derry.

I suggested somebody, and Eamonn said he wasn't good enough for Croke Park. When I said we have to win Ulster first, Eamonn reckoned there was no point in winning Ulster… if you don't win an All-Ireland.

He'd tell us you have to win in Croke Park and I always remember the conviction with which he said it. He had won a minor All-Ireland with Derry as manager in 1983 and he was very unlucky to have been beaten in an under-21 final in '85… and he had won his own minor and under-21 All-Irelands as a player.

He was always a bit miffed at the attitude of the senior players in his playing days and that it wasn't good enough. He wouldn't have personalised it, but he thought it could've been better.

Winning the '92 league against Tyrone was mentally *massive* for us… to go to Croke Park and win. The Meath game in the semi-final was my 12th game in Croke Park, and the first I had won. There was another mental block, albeit some of our boys had won minors and different things there. That league final was the perfect day for us. We won the cup and left Dublin with a chip on our shoulder. There was a function in Croke Park afterwards with everyone saying how unlucky Tyrone were.

We went up the road celebrating, and had a great night. We played them exactly two weeks later in the preliminary round of Ulster. We only won by three but we beat them off the pitch that day.

We backed that up with the Monaghan crash. We were 10-nil up and when Monaghan got a point before half-time, even the Derry crowd cheered. They hit three goals to come back and we got out of Castleblayney by the skin of our teeth, and won the replay with a bit to spare.

Then, to beat the All-Ireland champions Down in Casement, again that was a huge step. You had the All-Ireland champions meeting the National League champions and it was massive, not just for Derry, but for Ulster.

Beating Down wasn't a one off. We had beaten Meath and that was a big mental thing, they were still a big team. They'd won two All-Irelands and had been in a few finals, they were boys I looked up to.

They were all massive mental things, but losing the '92 Ulster final to Donegal was a huge kick where it hurts. There are games you regret letting go, but the two real kicks in my career were that game and losing to Down in 1994.

Those games hung over us and when Donegal won the All-Ireland, it gave us another kick. Down and Donegal had won Sam, we had won the National League. Now, it really was our time.

I HAD MISSED the start of the 1993 National League because I did my second cruciate. I played against Louth and then tore my cartilage in the week after the league quarter-final defeat to Donegal.

We threw that one away big time. It was another step back but it was possibly a blessing in disguise, it really created a focus. By the time we played Donegal in the Ulster final, it was the most focused week I have ever been involved in with a football team.

The last training, a Wednesday session at St Pat's Maghera back pitch… I remember there wasn't a ball dropped. It was ridiculous. People talk about the weather that day in Clones; we were never losing that game. Never, no matter what happened.

It was the only game in my life, where I would put by head on the block and say we were never going to lose. It was a build-up of those previous two years. It was thinking this was *our time* and we couldn't let it slip. We knew we had the work done. Mickey Moran's training was great and Eamonn had us in a serious mental place. The hurt was there, and we knew we were as good as what was there. It was now or never. It was a great coming together of heads, the whole county totally obsessed at that stage.

WE HAD A wall in our back yard… and you could only kick from the right side. There are two bricked up windows on it, and it suited me as a left footer. I would've practiced my frees up there.

In those days, when I was young, you had to hit all the frees off the ground. I wasn't particularly good… I just kept at it and kept at it.

I wouldn't been nervous coming into games, until I thought of my role as the team's free-taker. I knew the importance of the hard work from the other boys to get frees and you couldn't let them down. There was also the importance of free-taking in terms of winning games.

However, when the game started and anybody went near a free, I would've ripped the head off them to get taking it. I just *wanted* it. Whereas beforehand, I would ask myself why I kept putting myself through this.

Anthony and myself had a great relationship and we both knew I would go over into his territory when the wind was blowing from left to right, and he would come into mine, because it suited the way we naturally curled the ball.

We'd just nod at each other.

BEATING DUBLIN IN the semi-final was a mental thing, it was a win over one of the big teams… and it was in Croke Park. There was the build-up and the county was mad at that stage, it was obsessive.

I was a rep for the bank at the time and everybody – man, woman and child – wanted to talk about football. When I got up in the morning, my da had the paper read and was telling you what was in it. When you got home from training, he'd be asking how this one and that one was going. It was funny, you went to football to get *away* from football.

Everybody meant well, but, to this day, when I meet players, I don't ask them too much. I am lucky enough that I should know a bit about what they are thinking. While you don't want to sound disinterested, you don't want to be wrecking their heads.

The hype was non-stop coming into the final. There is still the massive euphoria of getting to an All-Ireland final, particularly with Derry's history, but you quickly start to think about Cork. The way my brain operates, it takes away a bit of the enjoyment of winning a game like an Ulster final because I very quickly began to think about the All-Ireland.

That's why that All-Ireland final, and the Sigerson final, are the only two competitions I won where there is no next game to focus on.

A lot of Derry people would talk about the semi-final being a bigger game than the final. To me, the final is still the *final*. The semi-final is no good if you don't go on and win the final. Whereas with the final, that's it... it's over.

Getting over Dublin was massive, but you soon realise you have to get tuned in for the final and, ultimately, we just knew we had to win it... and knew how hard it had been to get there. That was always in my head, looking back at what we'd done, who had beat us in the last three years... and we'd have to get out of Ulster again. And it transpired, with that Down team coming back again in 1994.

There was a great focus in that we were going in to play a Cork team that had played in four of the previous six finals, and had won two of them. *Who were we?* None of us had got remotely close. We got to a semi-final in 1987 but we weren't close, so you had to treat this as an opportunity of a lifetime. You were hoping there would be more, but as it turned out there wasn't.

After Joe Kavanagh's goal, the only consolation was that we had also been five points down at half-time against Dublin. It was Johnny McGurk's point that settled us... and there's no better man with the pressure.

Seamus Downey's goal put us on our way and we recovered very quickly, but Johnny's point was massive. If that five-point deficit had sat for five minutes, it might've been a more difficult thing to come back.

We were five down and playing with the breeze. That was fairly significant, but we were three up by half-time and it was game on.

I WENT INTO the final with a bit of a flu. On the Friday I didn't feel great. When I left home on the Saturday, I thought it was nerves. By the Sunday morning, it was getting worse and Dr Ben Glancy gave me a concoction to rehydrate me.

Then, 10 minutes into the second-half, just before John O'Driscoll's goal, I felt my legs going... but I just knew I had to dig in.

I didn't feel too well after the game either. I remember going up to do an interview in the press box in the top deck of the old Hogan Stand, and I was struggling to get up the stairs. The adrenaline got me through to the Thursday after the final. By the Friday morning I was in bed... and couldn't get out of it until the following Monday. I must've been bad if I missed out on my first weekend socialising in six months.

It's just shows you what adrenaline can do in a game when you need it.

People talk about the point I scored in the first-half of that final being from the wrong side, but that was the side I enjoyed kicking from because you were able to kick away from the defender, whereas if you were in the right corner with your left foot you had to kick across the defender.

I practiced a lot, basically going into that corner, because I couldn't get into the right corner. It wasn't a score I was going to take on but there weren't a lot of options. I looked up and was happy enough to have a pop at it with a bit of time on the ball. It is one of those ones that, if it goes over, you are a great fella... but if it goes wide, you were a coward after being involved in an off the ball incident minutes earlier.

We got a wee roll on them and the score I palmed over the bar after Gary Coleman's shot bounced down off the post came right on half-time.

At half-time, it was fairly calm. This was *our* opportunity. It doesn't stick out as one of the livelier changing rooms I have been in at half-time. We had an extra man and always knew from a couple of other occasions that Johnny was always the spare man. There were nights when there would be an extra man in training and we'd have used it for that scenario.

While our preparation wasn't at the level of teams in the modern game, we were as well a prepared team as there was anywhere in the 90s. That's not just in GAA, but right across the sporting spectrum. Everything that could've been done, was done.

AT THE FINAL whistle, it was absolute euphoria. I always remember Joe's words after the semi-final when we were walking up Clonliffe Road. We decided to get our heads cleared and head up to Quinn's, where we knew a lot of our mates would be, rather than being stuck on the bus.

His famous words were... '70 minutes from immortality'.

I said immortality was a bit strong, but he said if somebody wins 10 in-a-row, we'll always be the first... and that stuck in my ear.

At the final whistle, I was lucky enough to have the ball. Rooster (Fergal McCusker) was beside me, my own clubmate, and poor Don Davis came in to shake hands and got caught stuck in the middle of us hugging.

It was mayhem. You wanted to get out of the crowd... but you didn't want to get out of it. You wanted to soak up every absolute second of it. My uncle, Colum P Mullan, who had been paralysed in his prime at a young age, was in the wheelchair section under the Nally stand. Despite his disability, he had an incredibly positive attitude to get on with his life and achieve things, and was always an inspiration to me.

I ran over to him shortly after the final whistle. It was not something I had planned in advance, but I am so glad it entered my head to go to him through all the madness and it was a special moment to be with him. We wanted to soak it up, but then it was time to get into the cordoned off area for the presentation. We were soaked, but you don't even know what you are thinking. Joe always talks about it being an anti-climax, but not me. I don't get one percent of that. For me, I was on a high for months.

Growing up, I couldn't make a Derry minor squad when I was 17... when there were 18 other boys from my year at St Pat's on it, so I didn't think I'd ever play for Derry. Aside from that, I could never see Derry winning an All-Ireland because I could never see an Ulster team, never mind a Derry team, winning it. To put the two together and actually be on that Derry team, it was beyond comprehension in my head.

If you win a county title, a National League or an Ulster title, there is always another game to get ready for. That's why, to me, the 1993 final against Cork is the biggest game of my life.

For a lot of people, a club championship means as much and that's a big regret of mine that I didn't win one. I gave my mother my All-Ireland medal, and the rest of my medals are upstairs in a sweetie jar. You can't take away the memories... but I always said I would like to read through the paper clippings.

There was one day, seven or eight years ago, I saw the sweetie jar... and saw medals I'd forgotten... Division Three North when I started playing for Derry, intermediate championship medals from years and years ago. Someday, maybe when I am even older, I will read through the papers and clippings.

"

ENDA MULDOON

DERRY 1-12 ★ **ARMAGH 0-14**
Ulster MFC Quarter-Final
Athletic Grounds, Armagh
MAY 28, 1995

★ **DERRY:** D Hopkins; J Heaney, N Farren, M Kelly; P McFlynn, C McNally, D McNally; J McBride (0-1), G Doyle; G Coleman, **E Muldoon (0-7)**, A McGuckin; G Cushnahan (0-1), J Cassidy (1-3), D McErlain. **Subs:** P Wilson for McErlain, E McGilloway for D McNally.

★ **ARMAGH:** K Kimmons; P Watters, J McEntee, B Gordon; P Quinn, T McEntee, J Toal; B Duffy, P Oldham (0-3); P Loughran (0-3), S O'Hare (0-5), G Donnelly (0-1); J McGahan, A O'Neill (0-1), S McKeever (0-1) **Sub:** A Bennett for O'Neill.

66

LOOKING BACK AT my minor days, I suppose, for me, playing with the county never really came into it initially. I was just playing with the club. I had left school after fifth year, so I didn't play MacRory Cup or MacLarnon Cup football or anything like that really.

I sort of got lost. At the time, I was always asking myself if I was good enough to make county standard, with all the other boys playing school football in the MacRory or MacLarnon, whereas I was living in and playing for Ballinderry. I suppose I was leading a fairly sheltered life.

I was playing in goals for Ballinderry minors in 1993, as an under-16, and played full forward at my own age. The following year, I broke into the minor team at midfield, and in 1995 I was centre half-forward. Back in those days, Charlie

THE ACTION

★★★★★

LATE POINTS FROM Enda Muldoon and Joe Cassidy helped Derry fend off a strong Armagh challenge in their own backyard.

Cassidy's goal helped the wind-assisted Oakleafers into a 1-8 to 0-5 interval lead, but it took everything they had to hold on for a victory that began their march to the All-Ireland final.

Derry had a backbone of the St Patrick's Maghera's Hogan Cup winning team, with St Mary's Magherafelt winning the All-Ireland B title 12 months earlier, while Armagh had players from the MacLarnon Cup champions, St Michael's Lurgan.

It was nip and tuck for much of the first-half before Cassidy got clear to notch the only goal of the game on the cusp of the interval. Sean O'Hare and Philip Oldham hit points after the break for Armagh, and Barry Duffy began to get a handle on the game.

Cassidy kept the scoreboard ticking for Derry, and Muldoon chipped over two long-range frees that were the calling card of his summer to keep his side's noses in front.

Leading by a point, Derry went two clear with an injury time Muldoon score. Armagh did pull one back, but were unable to breach the visitors' defence to snatch a draw.

★★★★★

Conway and Mickey Donnelly would've been looking after our minor teams.

Everybody always talks about the unbelievable Ballinderry underage success at that time, with teams winning basically every competition on the way up. I wasn't in that group; there were about five or six of us who missed out on all of that. I did win titles with the under-12s and under-14s but didn't pick anything up after that at the under-16 or minor grades. We were beaten in two minor finals at that time by Bellaghy and Loup who went on to win Ulster.

Chris Brown took over the Derry minor team for the 1995 season. It was my final year of minor and Chris got in touch about coming to trials and, as they say, the rest is history.

I wasn't on the Derry panel the year before, but we played Bellaghy in the minor final down in Magherafelt. I was midfield that day, so maybe he spotted me and thought to himself, *Maybe I'll give this boy a shout.*

If I'm honest, I was a bit reluctant when I went to the Derry team at the start as I was probably going out of my comfort zone from anything I had been playing before that. From memory, I got on alright in the league. At the time, we were playing without anybody from St Pat's Maghera or the Convent (St Mary's Magherafelt) teams who were still involved in the MacRory Cup. Maghera went on to win the Hogan, with Magherafelt winning the All-Ireland B the year before.

We got on alright and I enjoyed it, so I stuck at it. We won a few games… we didn't win the league, but we did enough, and it gave us enough to build on. By the time we were getting ready for the championship, all the other boys filtered back in. There were eight Maghera lads, and Johnny McBride, Joe Cassidy and Paul McFlynn with the Convent, so that's a fair chunk of boys that wouldn't have played all through the league.

I'd say it was hard for the Derry management at the time because Maghera were dominant for those years, and they'd been holding all the cards. For me, I was just playing away at the football and none of that really bothered me, but I am sure it was hard on Chris and his management team of Paddy Crozier, Charlie O'Kane and Mickey Bradley.

I had a fair idea that we had a good team. There were loads of great players, the boys I knew and those I played against with St Pius and with the club. You don't know what other counties have, in terms of players, but I knew we had a strong enough squad with all the boys coming back from school duty.

FROM WHAT I can remember, there was big talk about that Armagh team. They had won Ulster the year before and were hot favourites to come through again, so it was a big ask for us to go into the Athletic Grounds and beat them.

I'd have played against the McEntees all through school when we played Abbey CBS, so we knew what we were coming up against. I marked Tony most of the time. He'd have been full-back and I would've been full-forward, that type of thing.

Playing Armagh, I suppose that was going to be a big, big battle and it was a massive win for us to get the season going. I had thought maybe that would've been the only minor game I'd have ever played to be honest. There was plenty of interest in it around Ballinderry at the time. There were a few of us playing… me, Adrian McGuckin, Paul Wilson, Gerard Cassidy and Declan McNally. When I think about it, they were brilliant times. There was great excitement and as a young boy playing at that level, and you think you are the man and that you've made it.

On the balance of my career, that was an important game because it was my first time playing in a big championship match in front of a big crowd. Back then, I wasn't too bad with nerves to be honest. I found that as I got older, and towards the end of my career, that I was more nervous because I would be thinking it was my last match and you'd put more pressure on yourself. When you were younger, it's just a football match… you just get on with it.

Derry seniors were All-Ireland champions two years before and there was a big following in the county. They were playing after us that day and there was a good crowd in for the game, so it was a great time to be playing with the minors. It was also a great summer that year with the weather, and I had just broken into the Ballinderry senior team at that time.

From that Armagh game itself, I only remember a few bits and pieces from it. I remember kicking over a few frees and that settled me into the game. We had a strong wind in the first-half and then we were sort of holding on at the end. The significance of it, for me, was that I had never played at that level before, and I wasn't sure if I was able for it. In that regard, it probably gave me the belief that I could be as good as anyone else if I put in the work and the effort.

I was marking Tony McEntee that day in Armagh and I was probably up against him three or four times before that. Chris played me at centre half-forward, and I was an outlet for a lot of our kick-outs that time as well. Johnny McBride and Doyler (Gary Doyle) were the midfielders, but they would sometimes pull to the wings the odd time and Hoppy (David Hopkins) would just hit me down the middle.

I always say that he was well ahead of his time. He was a great kicker and if you found space, he'd find you. It's not that we were doing much of that because the way the game was back then, the ball was usually just hoofed at that time. Hoppy, he had that low trajectory of a kick-out and he'd fit well into the game now.

I HAD ALREADY made my senior debut for Ballinderry as a goalkeeper against Ballinascreen in the 1994 McGlinchey Cup, so I was always used to kicking the ball off the ground. I'd say the kicking probably just came naturally to me, but don't get me wrong, I did put in a lot of work at it too. As the years passed, I fell out of favour for free-taking, because at club level Gerard Cassidy came on the scene and he was kicking them out of his hands, and I didn't really get kicking them anymore.

That summer of '95, in my first year with the seniors, I was still kicking a lot of the frees. It was between myself and Terence McGuckin, who also used to kick them off the ground. Looking back, that year was just brilliant. I got my first taste of playing for Derry in big games and I won my first senior championship with Ballinderry.

You couldn't have dreamt it. If you were writing it, you couldn't have written it better for a first year in football at adult level. We probably thought this is the way it is always going to be every year but, as we found out, it wasn't, and it was another six years until we won another championship with the club.

I had a great time with that bunch of Derry minor boys and a fair few of them went on to play for the under-21s when we won the All-Ireland in 1997. We had plenty of craic, there was no shortage of it with boys like Micheál Kelly and Gary Doyle, let me tell you. You couldn't have watched Doyle and those boys; they could have been up to anything.

There is no point in telling a lie, I would've had no real time for the Maghera boys at the start with the rivalry we had coming up through. We beat them in the D'Alton Cup final, when I was a First Year, but after that, they dominated the school scene. Then, as the Derry minor season went on, I began to get on very well with all those boys.

After beating Armagh, we had Tyrone in the semi-final and Adrian McGuckin scored two goals, and we went on to beat Down in the final. We played that unreal Galway team in the All-Ireland semi-final. They had Tomás Meehan, John Divilly, Michael Donnellan, Derek Savage and Padraic Joyce. That was a game I always remember from my career too, but I suppose the Armagh game in the first round was the defining one in that I was always asking myself if I could play at county level.

That Galway game was just brilliant; it was in Croke Park and there was a massive crowd in by the end of it.

It was a really good Galway team we beat, but we went on to lose to Westmeath in the final. No disrespect to them, but after beating such a brilliant team in the semi-final we shouldn't have let that one slip. That is a massive regret, it was brutal. Fair play to them, but we probably took our eye off the ball a bit after the Galway game. We probably got carried away. It is hard and young boys are easily influenced. People were going around tapping you on the back, telling you, 'You're the man' and things like that.

If you had to do it all over again, things would've been different between the semi-final and the final. I am not saying that about the management getting everything wrong. They probably had everything in place and done right. It was just that when we were out and about, and we were meeting people, they'd be telling us we were great, and you soon get carried away with it.

We won the All-Ireland two years later with the under-21s. We beat a great Meath team in the final and won all of our games quite easily. We had a few older boys on the team, like Sean Marty Lockhart, that wouldn't have played in the minor final. It was a different team, but I am sure if you ask any of the boys from our minor team, the '95 final and the defeat was probably in the back of their head and that we couldn't let this one slip.

THAT SEASON WITH Derry minors gave me a huge lift and it especially helped me with confidence. That came from a combination of factors - playing in front of big crowds with the best players in the county, and playing against the best teams in Ireland.

I would've always been quite shy, always sitting in the background. Anytime we were ever sitting in a room at a meeting, and somebody asked a question, I would've been at the back of the room… sliding as low down in the seat as I could so nobody would make eye contact.

Even now, I wouldn't be talking an awful lot, but I think the football has helped me. Even in my job in St Pius, coaching players and teams, it has helped me come out of myself a bit more. Before that, even on a night out, I wouldn't have been talking much to anybody… nearly just out there standing on my own.

That year with the minors was a great starting point for my career. People might say that we didn't win the All-Ireland senior with Derry. I am not saying that I wouldn't have loved to have won the All-Ireland. But, for the career I had and the people I met through it, I wouldn't change anything.

Maybe the one downside of it all… if I had to do it again, I'd have had a bit more balance in my life. Football totally dominated it and I never thought what happens when football ends.

I have a lot of friends from it all. From '95, if I hadn't have gone to the county minors, I might not have met the half of them and been stuck in my own wee bubble in Ballinderry thinking this is what it is, but there was so much more.

KIERAN McKEEVER

DUNGIVEN 0-14 ★ ERRIGAL CIARAN 1-8
Ulster Club SFC Final
St Tiernach's Park, Clones
NOVEMBER 9, 1997

★ **DUNGIVEN:** O McCloskey; S Heavern (0-1), **K McKeever**, S McGonigle; E Lynch, E McKeever, B McGonigle; B McGilligan, R McCloskey; P Murphy (0-1), E Kelly, R Murphy (0-1); J Brolly (0-3), G McGonigle (0-5), C Grieve (0-3). **Subs:** B Kealey for McCloskey, B Kelly for Brolly.

★ **ERRIGAL CIARAN:** C McAnenly; S Mallon, E McGinley, C McCann; E Kavanagh, C McRory, A McGinley (1-0); Pascal Canavan, H Quinn; B Neill (0-1), M McCaffrey, E McCaffrey; C Quinn, Peter Canavan (0-2), E Gormley (0-5). **Subs:** M McGirr for M McCaffrey, M Farrell for C Quinn.

66

WHEN WE LOST the 1996 county final to Bellaghy, we were very disappointed. We had high hopes going into that game, but looking back on it, maybe we were missing a wee bit of spark.

We had won the Ulster minor at St Paul's in 1990 and the players from that team had come in – Eoin 'Harry' McCloskey, Geoffrey McGonigle, and my brother Emmet brought a drive and hunger. Then we had younger players like Paul Murphy and Cathal Grieve who were starting to come at that time. They were only 18 but had toughness and also a will to win.

We knew if we could get a mixture of our experienced players and these boys that we'd be in with a good shout. We didn't think it would take as long, but it came to fruition in '97.

THE ACTION

★★★★★

FIVE POINTS WITHOUT reply and the harmony of their play saw Dungiven come from behind to land a first Ulster title. Dungiven came in as underdogs against a team who had chinned All-Ireland champions Crossmaglen in the semi-final. But it didn't matter.

Aidan McGinley blasted an early goal to the roof of the net but Dungiven never once reached for the panic button. They had leaders and performers in every line. Brian McGilligan and Ronan McCloskey held sway at midfield. Emmet and Kieran McKeever kept Peter Canavan and Eoin Gormley far enough from danger.

And their attack did the rest.

Joe Brolly and Geoffrey McGonigle may have been their assassins up top, but it was how Dungiven used them that made the difference.

Cathal Grieve wore No 15 but played everywhere. Player-manager Eugene Kelly thew himself on breaks, while Ryan and Paul Murphy kicked vital scores.

They were faced with the adversity of losing Brolly when the game hung in the balance.

It didn't matter. For the remaining 16 minutes, the Derry champions owned the game. They may have had to breathe a sigh of relief when goalkeeper McCloskey got a feint touch to a late Errigal goal chance, but it was Dungiven's day.

★★★★★

The younger players had loads of potential and the experienced guys gave it a bit of direction. At the same time, there was no hierarchy, and nobody was better than anybody else.

Everyone was involved in the craic and the slagging. Everybody took it and gave it as if they were the same age. That camaraderie came through in '97, more than it had done before.

The mixture was very good. The older boys were able to drive the young lads to a different level. They were good players but had never won a senior championship. The experienced men had done it in 91'and knew what it took, so that extra drive and push helped get us over the line.

Eugene Kelly was player manager. At times it felt as if it was all over the place and a bit disjointed, but it wasn't really. It was probably something that allowed the players to lead, and it meant we had leaders all over the pitch. That hadn't happened before.

Eugene picked Emmet as captain because the players who were in with Derry weren't training all through the year, so he wanted a club captain, and it worked out great. Emmet is very quiet but once he gets into the changing rooms, he is very motivating in the way he talks.

He led Joe Brolly and Brian McGilligan as if they were young boys like Cathal Grieve or Paul Murphy... everybody was the same. Everybody listened, everybody took it in and gave their bit. There was a really good bond that year.

Maybe it was building and maybe it was the defeat the year before that let us know we had to go an extra step, and everybody bought into it at that time.

WE NEEDED TWO games to beat Glenullin in the first round and both were played out in Drumsurn. I remember Dominic McIlvar gave me awful trouble in the drawn game and I didn't know what I was going to do.

We just scraped through because we kept nipping and battling and working. It was one of those games where we felt so lucky afterwards for getting through. It helped push us on a bit. Those were really good games and very tight. Glenullin were tough boys and you just had to find a way to beat them.

Those games stick with you because they are the ones that were hard to get over. We beat Magherafelt by five in the next game and it took two games to get over Lavey in the semi-final, so we were ready for the final.

We had great rivalry with Lavey all through the nineties. Most of them were good friends of mine from playing with Derry but the one thing you knew going onto the pitch, friendship stops at the gate.

Emmet and I had a wee saying, 'Cibé cad é a ghlacann sé' (whatever it takes) and with the McGurks and Downeys and indeed all Lavey players at that time, you knew you had to follow through on that saying. Lavey were All-Ireland club champions in '91, so beating them anytime gave us great belief. These were great games that helped build character.

As far as remember, we were quietly confident going into that final because we knew we had the beating of Castledawson. It was a matter of going out and performing to make it happen. That's not to take it away from them, but we just felt that way. We knew we had a good team and we'd been in the final 12 months earlier.

From the start, we knew we had man markers and we had scorers. Then, we had big Brian McGilligan in the middle of the pitch. We knew that, on our day, we could compete with anybody if everybody did their job.

Getting out of Drumsurn, from those two Glenullin games, was probably the kick in the backside that we needed to push us on. After that, it was just challenge after challenge.

WE THOUGHT ABOUT Ulster as soon as we had won the county title because clubs had gone and won it before us. Lavey had won the All-Ireland and then we knocked them out the following year. When you do things like that, there is always something in the back of your head that you can go on and win Ulster.

We knew we had a chance. There were big teams out there, like Errigal Ciaran and Crossmaglen, but we knew on our day we could beat anybody. That's the way we felt about it.

Some might say the St Paul's game in the semi-final was the toughest game, but I would never have thought of it that way. To me, winning is winning. It is supposed to be tough, and it is supposed to be a challenge.

I remember the win over St Paul's and how we had to fight to get out of it, but I always felt confident. It was a bit like playing Dublin and Cork with Derry in '93 when we went five points down in both of them, I never thought at any time that we were going to get beat.

It was a matter of getting the job done and trying to inspire. We had leaders, boys who could take it by the scruff of the neck and it mightn't have been the same person every week.

There were club players capable of doing it as well as somebody who was playing with the county. That's key, if you have belief in the players around you.

ERRIGAL WERE FAVOURITES because they had beat Cross, who were All-Ireland champions, and we knew that. We also knew that if Emmet could mark Eoin Gormley and I could mark Peter Canavan and we could get the ball up to Joe and Geoffrey, then we were in with a big shout.

Nobody was getting to mark Canavan only me. I always recall Eamonn Coleman coming to me after the '92 National League final and he had scored 1-2 off me. We were playing them two weeks later in the championship he came to me and suggested we'd put Tony Scullion on Peter.

I said: "no, you're not" and it didn't matter what he said, I was marking him.

It was hell for leather between myself and Peter in the club final that day in Clones, the same as every other day. We didn't have any real conversations but we had the utmost respect for each other off the pitch and on it but there were no holds barred on it, as it should be.

Peter's intensity, when he got the ball, you didn't see the movement because he was already gone. He had that intensity of turning right or turning left and David Clifford is now the same. You can only match that with the same intensity in the tackle. The minute you give a player like that one millimetre of space, he'll destroy you.

It was a mind game with me and Canavan. I was trying to get him to mark me as much as I was trying to mark him.

When a player like him wins the ball, your hands must be going at 100 miles an hour so he hasn't time to think about what he is going to do next.

Peter was about give and take and he was more about giving than taking. He'll not like me saying that but he was exactly like me, cibé cad é a ghlacann sé, he would've been first in there, yet people think defenders would always be the tough man in the battle.

Peter was one of those players, nothing fazed him, and he was as tough as nails with the skill oozing out of him, he was an amazing player, the best I ever marked and a real gentleman. I was lucky to be born in an era that I was able to go head-to-head with such quality.

When I was playing underage, going up from U-14, to U-16 and minor, I was centre half-back or midfield for Dungiven and I hit all the 45s.

In my senior days I always played centre half-back, midfield or centre half-forward, but that all changed in 1990. When Eamonn Coleman and Fr Sean Hegarty came in with Derry, they were trying to work from the back out and get the positions filled with a strong defence.

I remember Gary Coleman, Fergal P McCusker and different ones going into corner back and not wanting to play there really. I went in and gave it 100 percent every day and if I had been put in nets, I would've been the same there.

I was one of those people who just had to be the winner, so everything was a challenge. I had to be better than the other person. That's the way I was and it grew from then, but I was 23 or 24 before I played at corner back.

The time Coleman was going to put Scullion on Canavan, that was a complete insult because that was my challenge.

Coleman used to come to me two or three weeks before we'd play Tyrone and tell me that Canavan was up in Ballygawley saying he was going to score 1-5 off me. He was great at that and he would build you up to it.

Marking Canavan at club level, I suppose I didn't know what it was going to be like because it was completely different. He would've been playing with better players in the county team, they can think quicker and knew what he'd be doing. I didn't know if he was going to be better supported or less supported. It was his club so everyone knew him, so it was a bit of going into the unknown.

GOING IN TO play against Errigal, Eoin Gormley and Peter Canavan were the dangermen. We knew our other players would compete with their other players; they'd have the fight in the belly.

We had our own finishers and were lucky in a sense, in the balance we had. Geoffrey was like a big target man and you can hit the ball in on top of him and he'll compete.

Then, with Joe, you can fire it into the space and he'd win it, so we had two options up there. Not a lot of clubs would have that.

We knew we had Brian in the middle of the pitch, a huge presence with his frame. He could stop and be threat, he'd be able to turn players back.

I think we were confident going into that game and there was a massive buzz among the supporters because it was the first time the club had been in the Ulster final.

The fact that Eugene, Joe, Brian and myself had been on the Derry panel in '93, it meant we had been through all the euphoria of what a big game buildup looks like. We were able to manage the expectation and make sure people didn't get carried away with the buzz. We were able to keep grounded and that was important in it all.

Ryan Murphy and Cathal Grieve kicked great points that day. The young boys grew and they were the inspiration with scores that gave everybody a lift.

Then, when Joe went off injured, it didn't faze us. We didn't have a gameplan like you'd have now, where everybody nearly knows where to stand at. It was different then, you just competed for a ball.

I never felt like we were going to be beat even though ten minutes into the second half, we were still behind. You need to have that focus and belief. We kicked four or five points in a row and we became the complete team in that period of time. Everyone seemed to click and we were all on the same wavelength at that point. Everybody was on the front foot and knew what they were doing, and it just happened from there.

It was one of those things you take a lot pleasure from. Sometimes when you are out on a pitch, it can be a very lonely battle but when something like that happens it is a completely different feeling.

You come out and win a 40-60 ball and just know somebody is coming off your shoulder, you could nearly sense it and know they are going to be there.

Errigal did get their early goal, but we didn't show any signs of panic. In getting to the final, we were confident in ourselves.

We had talked about it all week and all year. We had to keep 15 men on the pitch, be fighting to the bitter end and for every ball. To this day, that's still relevant no matter what gameplan you have and then the cream comes to the top if everybody has a 100 percent workrate.

Everybody believed it was going to be our day. Even at half time, even though we were behind, everything was calm.

Eugene gave a talk. Danny Quinn gave a talk. Myself and McGilligan also spoke. It was calm, inspirational and motivational.

It was all about getting focussed and the message was how we were the better team but hadn't played to our potential. We knew if we went out in the second half and played to our potential, then we'd get it over the line.

Everybody was saying it and believed it. Like we did all year, at the start of every game and at half time, we all got into a circle and put our hands in, it was one for all and all for one.

McGilligan won the throw in at the start of the second half and it went from there. Brian had lost his mobility. He had bad knees at that stage and he wasn't as powerful a runner, but he could still jump and he could still knock boys out of the road.

We had Eoin McCloskey in nets and he had a great kick-out. He could kick the ball 70 yards. That's a great relief when you can release the tension from a defence and have time to settle yourself. It meant a lot in football at that time.

When I think back on the first half, yes it was tight and there were plenty of heavy tackles going in, but it wasn't dirty, I would've said it was really tough. Everybody was trying to find their feet and see who was boss.

Late on, we were three or four points up but it was far from comfortable. I felt it was never over until it is over. The thing about Errigal Ciaran and their threat, they could've scored a goal at any time and you can't switch off.

I found that from marking Canavan. If you lost concentration for a split second, he would've turned you inside out. Concentration had to be your greatest asset in the game, the minute you lose concentration...he is gone.

I'll tell you what winning a battle with Canavan looks like...I wouldn't have known what he had scored, and I didn't care. I went to win every ball, what happened with the last ball didn't matter... you couldn't change it. If he got a point, it didn't bother me. It was the next ball that was the most important, it had to be won no matter what, that was my father's teaching.

I didn't look at what someone scored. Every ball was different and a different challenge you had to win.

I was a great believer in the days of the old traditional corner-back. The blanket defence took a lot of the art of tackling out of the game, but coaches are now starting to realise you still need man markers. If you don't have someone to man mark good players like Clifford then you can't control the game.

Whenever that half-back on the other team was on the ball, you knew what his options were. If there is all this space on a certain side for the forward to run into, what do you do? I looked at it differently. I knew that if I went in front of him, with my hand on my man, then the half back is going to see me and change the direction of the play. That would be my job done and I would step back to see what was needed the next time.

A lot of defenders play alongside or behind and it is too safe an option at times. You have to go and win the ball or at least get the hand in and make a player go a second time. You can't allow him to get the ball as you're going to foul him in a scoring position or you'll have to play the percentage at that stage.

WINNING THAT DAY, it was euphoria. I couldn't believe it. Us, our wee club, had won an Ulster title. It was an unbelievable feeling and that's why this game is the one for me.

First and foremost, we are all club people and community people. That is a big thing in my life. It always has been and it's actually massive right now. I live and breathe this club and the community.

Locally, it's the GAA that looks after the community. During Covid, we had food banks, hot dinners to people, pharmacy runs, coal, oil and turf. All for those most vulnerable.

I believe that the GAA has been the driver for peace and putting it into practice on the ground in the north and that going forward we can be the leaders in achieving a thriving, settled, equal society in an Ireland for everyone.

I'll give you an example. Joe Brolly and I, we grew up together and played football and hurling in the same age group.

We remain friends to this very day, no matter how many times he falls out with me. I was streetwise and he wasn't with being in a boarding school most of his life.

He used to rely on me and speak to me in confidence about things and he still does. He'd ring me up and that's not because of being on the same county team, that's about the club. There are other examples around the town where my friends are still my friends. That, to me, is important and that's what made up my mind which game was the most defining one, even ahead of some of the big games with Derry. I always remember beating Meath in the '92 league semi-final as the start of our successful run. Without the club, there can be no county. The communities within the GAA, singularly and collectively, are massive. It is one of the greatest organisations in the world and it hasn't been given the recognition it deserves.

Winning that Ulster title, it can't be put into words what it meant to the men who built this club. They are part of it and we feel it belongs to them as much as it does to the players. That's what makes it massive.

That's the last championship we won and, to this day, those men are fighting and debating and trying to get the structures in place and create the conditions for other teams to do what they did.

That's how important it is, and we do all this voluntary. It's a passion, it's community, it's culture, it's who we are, it's that important to us.

Some people, if they are awake 18 hours of the day, they are naturally thinking about their club for 17 of them. That's what makes pride in the club and the community. It is for everyone and not just you as an individual.

Derry is different. Derry belongs to Derry and you are part of it. The '93 boys were together for the 25th anniversary and we're getting together for the 30th.

Not everybody will be there, the spectators who won it with you, they are not there. With the club, you have it every day of the week. That's the difference.

THERE IS A regret we didn't win the All-Ireland that year... 100 percent. Corofin were great champions, there is no doubt about it, but we played with 14 men for most of that All-Ireland semi-final.

I felt we let ourselves down and I feel we could've done more on the day. I think playing with 14 men played on some players' minds. Every run became tougher because there was a lot of backtracking, and they couldn't get back up the pitch again. I think they were consumed by the negativity of being a man down.

We still had two great forwards up there that could score. They put two men on Joe that day and Geoffrey couldn't get enough of a supply of the ball.

We ended up getting beat by two points and Corofin went on to win it. Going in to play Erin's Isle in the final, it would been the same as going into the Errigal Ciaran game, we had the man markers and we had the scorers.

We knew we'd beat Erin's Isle; it was just about getting over Corofin but it wasn't to be. It was very, very disappointing. I was never as disappointed in all my life. That was a game we should have won, it hurt and it still hurts.

”

SEAN MARTY LOCKHART

DERRY 1-7 ★ DONEGAL 0-8
Ulster SFC Final
St Tiernach's Park, Clones
JULY 19, 1998

★ **DERRY:** E McCloskey; K McKeever, **SM Lockhart**, G Coleman; D O'Neill, H Downey, P McFlynn; A Tohill, E Muldoon; G Magill (0-2), D Dougan (0-1), E Burns (0-1); J Brolly (1-2), S Downey, J Cassidy (0-1). **Subs:** D Heaney for Burns, E Gormley for S Downey, G McGonigle for Cassidy.

★ **DONEGAL:** T Blake; B McGowan; JJ Doherty, M Crossan; D Diver, N Hegarty (0-1), N McGinley; J McGuinness, M Coll; J Duffy (0-1), A Sweeney (0-1), J Gildea; M Boyle, T Boyle (0-3), B Devenney (0-2). **Subs:** J Ruane for Crossan, J McHugh for Sweeney, B McLaughlin for M Boyle.

66

IT WAS MICKEY Moran who gave me the first call into the Derry senior squad. I left St Patrick's College Maghera in June of 1995 and Mickey asked me onto the panel in August, ahead of the autumn stages of the National League.

I was 19 when I joined the panel and my first game was against Kerry in Ballinascreen and by that stage Brian Mullins, God rest him, had been installed as the new manager. I played part of that campaign in a wing half-forward role, and I have no idea really where that came from. Throughout school, I played full-back or centre half-back but Brian had me working up and down the field as a defensive half-forward.

We won the National League that season, defeating Mayo in the semi-final and Donegal in the final. Martin Shovlin, playing at left half-back on the day of

THE ACTION

★★★★★

IT WAS THE late, late show for Derry as Joe Brolly's goal grabbed victory from the jaws of defeat after a low-scoring encounter in damp conditions. Derry, with Brian Mullins as manager, came into the final after controversially losing to Cavan 12 months earlier and it was a tight battle that saw the sides level at half-time, 0-3 all, and four times in total.

The Oakleafers were four-point semi-final winners over Armagh, after easing past Monaghan in the first round. Derry had a new swathe of players from their All-Ireland under-21 winning team of 1997, but it looked like they were going to be outfoxed. Midway through the second-half, the game looked like it had swung in Donegal's favour when John Duffy fisted a Manus Boyle free to the net, but it was ruled out for square ball.

Brendan Devenney was lively for Donegal, but Sean Marty Lockhart kept Tony Boyle away from the scoring zone. When Gary McGill levelled the game at 0-7 each, a draw was very much on the cards before Donegal nosed in front again. Then came the final play.

A scuffed McCloskey kick-out was hoovered up by Paul McFlynn, who was fouled. Anthony Tohill lamped the free forward, where Geoffrey McGonigle muscled his marker off the ball to put the winning goal on a plate for Brolly.

★★★★★

the final, marked me in what was my first game in Croke Park.

As a young player coming into the set-up, you get advice from the more experienced men like Damian Barton, Kieran McKeever, Tony Scullion and Gary Coleman, players who had immense experience playing on the big days. Their advice was supportive and encouraging, whereas Brolly, who was playing at right corner-forward, told me, whilst pointing to the area in front of him, to stay the hell out of that space… so I wouldn't get in his way whilst he was trying to get the ball.

When I joined the squad, the defence still comprised the '93 men, who were formidable defenders, so as a 19-year-old rookie, I wasn't ready to play in defence. During a league game against Clare, they tried me on Gerry McInerny and he skinned me, scoring 1-3 from play. After the match, one of the '93 boys tapped me on the back and said, 'Welcome to inter-county football Sean Marty… your hard work starts now'.

It was a great bit of advice; I knew then I had a lot of hard work ahead of me. It was hard to break into the back six and it took me two or three years to settle into that defensive role; I just wasn't good enough at the start.

Tyrone beat us in the '96 championship, but we got to the final the following year and Cavan pipped us by a point. I was playing wing half-back and it was my man, Raymond Cunningham, who scored the 'wide point' that day. In 1997, we won the under-21 All-Ireland. Danny Quinn, Brian McGilligan, Eugene Kelly and Harry Gribbin were the management team. At that time, there was a good senior team and a raft of boys coming through from St Patrick's Maghera, and other boys like Enda Muldoon, Joe Cassidy, Johnny McBride and Paul McFlynn.

Looking back, we had a good squad then. We trained away with both the under-21s and the seniors, it was a balancing act. Nowadays, you have to train for one team or the other. There are county managers who want to hold onto their under-21 players. Brian Mullins was very accommodating and gave Danny access to us to prepare for up-coming games. The arrangement worked well, as Danny was also a member of the senior management team and they had a good working relationship.

We beat Fermanagh in the under-21 Ulster final, Mayo in the All-Ireland semi-final and Meath in the final. A Meath team who had three or four boys who had won senior All-Ireland medals the year before.

That fed into the UUJ Sigerson Cup squad the following year, with Adrian McGuckin at the helm. There was a good squad of Derry boys in the set-up, many of whom came through St Patrick's College under the guidance of Adrian. I remember the 1997-98 Sigerson campaign. I was on my year out from university and I was working with Derry County Board coaching hurling throughout the county. After work, I would drive to Toome, meet Adrian around half four and head up to Jordanstown. I would've got home at around half ten at night.

I was following that routine two or three times a week, as well as county training. We got to the Sigerson final that year. We beat the Guards in the quarter-final; they had Johnny Crowley playing for them. It was Queen's in the semi-final, who had Cormac McAnallen, God rest him, and then we lost to Tralee in the final against a star-studded team, including, Seamus Moynihan, Padraic Joyce, Michael Donnellan and Jim McGuinness.

It was an unbelievably intense year but it would prove to be my most successful. The heavy workload over the winter of '97 proved to be beneficial later in that '98 season; I was flying fit and we were playing at the highest level. As well as the Sigerson Cup, we were playing in Division One of the National League and were preparing for the Ulster Championship.

On a personal level, I cemented my place in the Derry defence, won the Ulster title, was named Ulster Player of the Year, represented Ireland in the Compromise Rules, was awarded Irish player of the series and, in addition, I received an All Star.

In retrospect, I was in a kind of a bubble, concentrating on training and preparing for the next match. I don't think I really appreciated what I had achieved at the time. I am grateful to my parents, my club Banagher and my teachers in St Patrick's, Adrian McGuckin and Paul Hughes for their influence in keeping me grounded and humble.

WE LOST TO Offaly in the 1998 league final. We had five or six under-21s in the team and I remember Offaly playing with a two-man full-forward line of Vinny Claffey and Roy Malone. Kieran McKeever marked Claffey, and I picked up Malone.

At the start, when you came on the scene, there were so many of the 1993 All-Ireland winners there; you are the youngest in the changing room and you are in awe of them. Big Anthony is there, Henry Downey, Danny Quinn, boys like that. As they moved on, I became a middle player and then the experienced player. It was a privilege, an unbelievable privilege.

McKeever, Downey and Scullion were continually giving me advice, so I was getting advice from the best defenders in Ireland. I took their advice on board and developed myself as a defender.

A lot of young lads now make a county squad and they think they've made it but they haven't. Your hard work only starts then, because it is so tough and competitive at that elite level.

Having reached the '98 league final, we were going into that Ulster Championship as favourites. In the quarter final, we scored 3-13 against Monaghan, and 2-13 against Armagh in the semi-final. However, Donegal proved to be very strong defensively so we only managed to score 1-7 in the final but it was enough to secure the title.

In the weeks leading up to the final, defenders were matched up against the danger men of the opposing team. For the final, I was given the job of marking Tony Boyle, who came with a big reputation.

You had between 10 days and two weeks to prepare and get the head right for what was coming and, thankfully, there was a lot of video footage of Tony playing previous games.

I studied the videos and at training I got Brolly to re-enact his moves whilst I would mark him. I was pre-empting what Tony would do in the final and visualising how I would close him down. In addition to the work at Owenbeg, I put in a lot of work on Banagher pitch, visualisation and running out to the side where I wanted to shepherd Boyle.

ON THE DAY of the final, he walked over to me, and Tony looked a lot different to Brolly... bigger, stronger and quieter. Boyle had an All-Ireland medal; he was an All Star and he was my first major challenge at that level. He scored two points that day and won a lot of ball out in front, but he never got past me because of my tackling preparation. At the start of the game, I was nervous, but when the first ball came in and I got a fist to it, I settled, got the measure of him and grew in confidence.

Boyle was great at getting out in front, he was a very intelligent player, he read the game well and had good ball control. Back then, there wasn't as much emphasis on strength and conditioning and when I look back at the photographs of me tackling Boyle... he was a strong, well-built 31-year-old county player, and

I was a skinny, scrawny 21-year-old.

The wet day helped me too… wet days help defenders with the skid and bounce of the ball. The forward doesn't have the same control with handling. I knew then that I wasn't going to get on the ball or set up play, my job was just to mark him.

From that day on, I always relished the challenge of marking the best forward on the other team. It always motivated me when people told me, 'It can't be done'… it made me want to prove them wrong. It made me prepare harder and more diligently to prove the point.

It was 0-3 each at half-time in Clones, and I remember going in soaking. We were squelching as we walked, so I changed the socks and shorts before going back out to be that bit fresher. In those days, you had the longer jerseys and they were as heavy as hell.

I suppose that game, in the end it came down to a bit of grit, determination and character. Sometimes football goes out the window.

You have to give Donegal credit. They shepherded our forwards that day. We had Seamus Downey, Joe Brolly, Enda Gormley, Dermot Dougan, Gary McGill, Joe Cassidy… and Donegal did well at the back.

I remember they came out and went a few points ahead of us in that second-half, but those last 10 minutes were a flash and it came down to the crucial winning goal. I remember looking on as Tohill kicked it long over the top and into Geoffrey. There was a slight push and he put it into Brolly, and he made no mistake to score the goal.

One of the things I always laugh about from that day, but wasn't shown on TV, was when Donegal hit a quick kick-out after our goal. I turned and Eoin McCloskey, our goalkeeper, who was a fireman, was standing on top of the crossbar facing into the crowd and still celebrating the goal. McKeever had to roar up at him, 'Eoin, get the f**k down here'… as Donegal were on the attack.

They got a goal disallowed in the second-half with John Duffy fisting it into the net, and some people might say we were fortunate to win that day, but that's the way it goes. We went to Magherafelt for the celebration after the match but it was a quiet enough affair because success was expected back then. Compare that to the buzz and excitement after the last two Ulster finals.

Unfortunately, we were beaten by Galway in the All-Ireland semi-final that year. We weren't good enough on the day, but three years later, in 2001, we were good enough, but let it go in the last 10 minutes. We were five points up going into the final stretch but didn't manage the game to the final whistle.

THE MODERN-DAY GAME, with defensive structures, doesn't allow for as many mouth-watering duels between top class forwards and defenders. Throughout my career, I had the privilege of marking some of the best forwards in the game in 50 yards of space… with no sweepers.

Personally, I feel that defenders are not exposed enough to that one-to-one battle and when they get to the latter stages of the All-Ireland, Croke Park is a very unforgiving environment if you are not adept at man-to-man marking.

The modern-day defender is expected to attack, set up play and score. I feel there is a need for at least two defenders, who are specialist man-to-man markers in each team. A good example of this is the Dublin team under Jim Gavin, when he had the luxury of four of his back six being proficient man-markers. This contributed to him achieving five in-a-row.

These great duels are what make our games unique and exciting to watch, the likes of Michael Fitzsimmons and David Clifford, Keith Higgins and James O'Donoghue… and in hurling, you've TJ Reid and Sean Finn.

Nowadays, teams have their own video analysts who, armed with specialist software, can analyse and break down the strengths of the opposition. Players are then handed the data to work from. Back then, I had to source the footage myself… those big VHS tapes, and sit at the video recorder with the stop, rewind and play buttons… and make my own notes. I found that gave me an incredible insight into my opponent and this, coupled with a phenomenal work ethic, worked for me.

However you prepare for your game, whether you are a defender, midfielder or forward, put in the hard work, strive to improve your game and remember to relish the challenge when people tell you… 'It can't be done!'

PAUL McFLYNN

LOUP 0-11 ★ BALLINDERRY 0-7
Derry SFC Final
Celtic Park, Derry
OCTOBER 12, 2003

★ **LOUP:** S McGuckin, J Young, Joe O'Kane, P McGuinness; B Lavery, P O'Kane, F Devlin (0-1); J McBride (0-1), John O'Kane; B McVey, F Martin, R Rocks (0-3), **P McFlynn (0-2)**, S McFlynn (0-3), P Young. **Subs:** E McQuillan (0-1) for McVey, S Doyle for Martin.

★ **BALLINDERRY:** M Conlan; C Wilkinson, N McCusker, K McGuckin; P Wilson, R McGuckin, D Crozier (0-1); D Conway (0-1), J Conway (0-1); C Gilligan, B Conway, A McGuckin (0-1); D Bateson, E Muldoon (0-2), F Muldoon. **Subs:** J Bell for R McGuckin, S Donnelly for Gilligan, M Harney for F Muldoon, G Cassidy (0-1) for B Conway, C Devlin for Bateson.

66

AFTER WINNING THE 1993 and '95 Ulster Minor Championships, it took 10 years for the first batch of us to come through and win a senior championship. The '95 win coincided with Loup's first year in senior football, after winning the intermediate league and championship double.

We got to the senior semi-final that year and were beaten by Ballinderry, who went on to win it. At that stage, you were naive and thought it was pretty easy and it wouldn't be long until we'd be in a final and we'd be winning one.

That first year was really fairytale stuff with the momentum kicking on from underage.

We also had a very good manager in Martin Coyle. He was a really good motivator, with the young boys really responding and was one of the reasons why

THE ACTION

★★★★★

LOUP ENDED A 67-year wait for a Derry senior title with victory over neighbours Ballinderry. The Shamrocks, All-Ireland champions in 2002, were in pursuit of a third successive title, having swatted Loup aside 12 months earlier, holding them to half a dozen converted Ronan Rocks' frees in a 1-11 to 0-6 defeat.

But this was different. With Malachy O'Rourke and Leo McBride at the helm, Loup were primed. When Paul McFlynn's left-footed score in the opening minutes sailed over, it set the tone. Points from Enda Muldoon and Adrian McGuckin had Ballinderry ahead, before Shane McFlynn fired over to tie the scores with 10 minutes to the break. An Adrian McGuckin point edged the holders back in front by the 18th minute before Shane McFlynn fired over in the 20th minute to level the scores at 0-3 each.

With Rocks and the McFlynn brothers notching two points each, Loup were 0-6 to 0-3 in front at half-time. It was their time. The underage groundwork under the direction of Colum Rocks had a group of players assembled, with O'Rourke taking over from where Patsy Forbes left off at the end of the 2002 with a league title.

Loup were always able to keep a grip on the game and when a tame penalty shout fell on deaf ears late on, the writing was on the wall. Leading by three points, they kept their heads to manage the game before a late Paul McFlynn free clinched the title.

★★★★★

we did so well in '95. He stayed until 1996 or '97 and after that we plateaued for various reasons.

Maybe we didn't have the right management teams in place and it still hadn't really sunk into boys what was needed to kick on to the next level. Boys thought, with natural ability and doing what we had always done, we'd get there, but we didn't.

Colum Rocks had taken groups that had won under-14, under-16, minor… and all the way up through. A lot of the players had won schools' titles. They were used to success and the ability was there in abundance, but because you were from a club who had played junior, intermediate and now into senior football, you are trying to make a breakthrough to the so-called big boys… the likes of Dungiven, Lavey and Bellaghy at that time.

We hadn't realised the work that it took and that bit of extra commitment needed to get us to that level.

Martin Coyle's brother, Malachy, took us in 2001 and it ended on a downer against Lavey in the championship. We went in as slight favourites against a team who, by their own admission, were in decline. That was a bit of a set-back because we had a really good league campaign that year. We had beaten Ballinderry and beat Bellaghy with Malachy doing a really good job, but when it came to the championship it all fell to pieces.

I remember Henry Downey coming into the changing rooms after it and telling us Lavey shouldn't have been beating us and we were full of talent. He said how they were chasing another championship with an aging team and we were ripe. People might've thought he was patronising, but he was telling the truth and the one thing about Henry was that he was honest. Even though we had made progress, it was disappointing. There was a bit of a culture change in terms of commitment and that was needed, and Malachy brought discipline to the set-up.

I remember driving home, wondering how we had got it wrong? On reflection, we had only put it all in for one year and there was an improvement.

When Patsy Forbes came on board in 2002, he took it to another level we didn't know existed in terms of discipline and structure. Patsy doesn't drink and wasn't one for putting heavy drink bans on boys, but he tailored training for early on a Sunday morning and there wasn't much scope for boys going out the night before.

There were boys hanging around the panel for years, doing a bit of training but not wanting to fully commit. By a natural process of commitment, he got rid of some of them, basically telling us, 'You're either with us, or without us'. Boys who had been playing senior ended up in the reserves, and it was a real gunk to them and some then got back into the senior team.

That 2002 final was our first final and it was a case of a lot of boys freezing on the day.

There was a lot of hype and expectation around the community. When you look back, Ballinderry were coming off the back of being All-Ireland club champions.

On the night we beat Glenullin in the semi-final down in Lavey, they had won their semi-final on the Saturday and I remember a conversation with Gerard Cassidy and Sean Donnelly.

We had just stepped into the Lavey clubhouse and Gerard said, 'We'll beat you by six or seven points, no bother'… and I remember Donnelly, who is now my brother-in-law, grabbing him by the arm and trying to get him out of there before he said much more.

There was a bit of craic, but they did mean it and they proved it by beating by us by eight points.

Part of their team talks that year centred around none of the teams having a Colin Corkery… that was their attitude after having beaten Nemo in the All-Ireland.

The management told us to take the inside line behind the band before that final, closest to the crowd. It was one of those things you do to get a psychological edge, but we ended up behind the Ballinderry flag. I remember Donnelly shouting, 'Lads, they've never been here before, they don't know where they should be'… and that type of thing didn't faze them.

We were bitterly disappointed, but we went on to win the league, so there was something left to play for that year.

That was our first senior title as a club and I remember our trainer Marty McElkennon talking about how important it would be if we wanted to make it a stepping stone. It was the first time we beat Bellaghy at senior level in a meaningful competition, so there were plenty of positives from that year.

PATSY STEPPED DOWN after telling us he'd be there for one year at most, and he left us in a really good position. We ended up getting Malachy O'Rourke and Leo 'Dropsy' McBride on board about March of the following year. My da was chairman at the time and few of the players went with him to meet them at the Gables restaurant in Dungannon.

We didn't want to rush and, in the past, we'd have taken a manager for the sake of getting someone. Marty McElkennon recommended him and said we'd hear a lot more about O'Rourke over the years. He said about him being a good football man, but, above all else, the most genuine man you'd meet.

Malachy was asking us loads of questions and wanted to know who our leaders were. We were starting to doubt if we'd convinced him, but within a few days they rang to accept the job.

I remember playing with Derry in a championship match that year; we drew with Tyrone in Clones and they hammered us in the replay the following Saturday. We had a game against Ballinascreen on the Sunday... we weren't going that well in the league. I gathered that Malachy and Dropsy were thinking about whether they were going to walk away or not.

We won really well and they saw something that night, putting it down as a turning point and it went from that.

I remember us having a meeting one night about setting targets and everyone saying we wanted to win the championship. The draw had paired us with Lavey, who we had never beaten. Malachy brought us all down to reality, telling us the only objective we needed was to beat Lavey in the first round.

Every week of that year, Lavey were mentioned in some way and everything was geared towards that. If we were beaten in a league game, it didn't matter. It was about learning and performing and improving for Lavey.

O'Rourke got his hands on the 2001 match report, when they beat us, reading snippets out of it and putting bits up on the wall. We had never come across anything like that before. He was asking us what the paper was going to say on the Monday morning. Would it be the same old story, or would we write our own script?

Like all the games that year, Malachy always had us quietly focused, without it being crazy. That came from being drip-fed about Lavey... and we beat them by nine or 10 points, the first time we turned them over.

We beat Kilrea in quite a drab affair, 0-10 to 0-6, after not playing overly well and when we beat Glen in the semi-final, the first mention of Ballinderry came after their win over Slaughtneil.

While they had walked over us the year before, it didn't hamper our confidence. We had moved on in terms of our belief, but it was there as a source of motivation.

From the 2002 final, there were ratings out of 10 done in the paper. O'Rourke pulled that out and read a few of them. I remember him reading mine out. I was captain and it said how I did well and got a seven, but the last line was… 'Needed to get more from him'.

On the week of a game, he'd deal with the opposition on a Tuesday. He'd go through the latest team, any permutations of who might come in, all their strengths and weaknesses. Then on the Thursday, it was always about us.

I remember him reading out a phrase from the 2002 final and how Niall McCusker came out and scattered the Loup forwards 'like confetti', which he did do. It also referenced that we hadn't scored from play, something that had been thrown up against us anyway, and we knew were going to have to change that.

Under O'Rourke, if you weren't a worker, you didn't play. There were boys that didn't start particular games because, in his eyes, they weren't working hard enough in the role and weren't doing enough off the ball to warrant a place. He changed the team slightly, moving me into the forward line as a third midfielder. Padraig O'Kane came to centre half-back and his brother, Joe was in at full-back in his first year of senior football.

Ballinderry were going for three in-a-row and that was a big thing. The rumour was that they had their flags made… thankfully, they didn't have a chance to get them out. It was one of those days when you know you can do it, but you know it is going to take a massive performance to get over the line.

That was testament to O'Rourke; he had us believing and not going in with hang-ups.

We always met on a Saturday, togged out and warmed up, with a bit of shooting for about half an hour… and there would be another brief meeting. I remember being relaxed but focused. I always look back on games when you had the same feeling, and days when you were overhyped and didn't perform.

O'Rourke always recognised the need to lighten the mood because if you are too tense you end up inhibited, and you don't do yourself justice.

THERE WAS SO much attached to that one game, it had been 67 years since Loup had won a championship. I ended up scoring the first point of the game with my left foot. Someone off-loaded me the ball and I was solo running through the middle. Ronan McGuckin was trying to usher me onto my left and I was running out of room. Somebody was coming in, so I just kicked it and it went over the bar.

It got us settled and scoring one with the left was a real confidence booster for me. I remember Brendan Conway, an uncle of Darren and James from Ballinderry, who was married into the Loup, putting his arm around me that night and asking where I got the left foot from?

I also remember my brother Shane being nervous that morning, but I told him everybody was the same. The work was done, and it was about relaxing and going out to play our normal game. He went out that day and got the better of Niall McCusker. He hit three points and I remember the one he got from play; it was a big diagonal ball into the square. Nine times out of 10, Niall is gobbling those up and scattering a few boys on the way out.

Shane caught it, Niall was wrestling with him, but he swung it over the bar and that was a huge confidence booster for him, and another statement for the team that we were not going to get pushed around. We played with the breeze and were 0-6 to 0-3 up at half-time. We were 30 minutes away but knew what Brian McIver would've been saying in their dressing-room and, in their eyes, they hadn't started.

Looking back, we were never in any danger of losing. They did hit a few scores and I remember thinking we needed to get our hands on the ball. Whatever way Shane McGuckin kicked out the ball, the midfielders spread and it went straight to me. I went on a bit of a solo and I could see Johnny McBride going past me. I slipped it to him and… BANG… over the bar from 40 yards into the breeze. I thought to myself, that's it. It was a killer score.

I remember Finty Devlin going up and kicking a point, and you just knew then.

There was a Ballinderry penalty appeal with three points in it. Darren Crozier had three or four men around him and he went down, not very theatrically, but some referees would've given it. My heart was in my mouth, but when Bruno (referee Adrian McGilligan) flagged a free out, I remember the relief. We played a few more minutes and there was the final free, about 20 yards out.

O'Rourke had introduced us to the TCUP concept – thinking correctly under pressure. When I got that free, TCUP was the only thing I was thinking. I was doing a bit of it on the frees, visualisation, closing my eyes and seeing it going over the bar. When I put that one over, the fist went up... we had done it.

IT WAS PANDEMONIUM and people were coming all roads and directions. Malachy did say that if we won it, we'd take time on the pitch to savour it.

There were the special moments on the pitch. Meeting Shane, mammy, daddy and my younger sister, Karla... they are priceless and you don't want to go home. When everything settled down, the presentation had taken place and when people dispersed, Malachy got us into a huddle. The cup was there in the middle, on the grass. I was looking at it and couldn't get my head around this.

Malachy talked quite calmly about the fact we did what most people outside the circle felt we couldn't. He was hammering home the sense of togetherness and spirit that was central to what we did. When he made that speech, you believed him even more and he used it as an opportunity to say, 'Lads, this year is not over yet'... and that we'd think about Ulster later. It hadn't entered anybody's head, we had no right to think that way – until then.

We walked in with the cup very quietly, there was nothing like you'd see now with roaring and shouting because we'd done that all out on the pitch.

It was a different bus journey from going home in 2002, literally day and night with that sense of anticipation of walking into the club and the significance of what we'd done. The 67 years, the generations who went before, all the emotion and all the children being there.

Nobody was carrying beer off the bus... Malachy told us we were going in as ambassadors for the club. That's how you had to behave until the formalities were over, then we could do whatever we wanted. Louis McAlynn, God rest him, was the bus driver and he dropped us off on the road just outside the pitch.

There was music playing, bagpipes and fireworks going off. People were lined all the way to the club; it was one of those moments where you want to stand still and take it in. I remember seeing Joe Devlin, God rest him, who would've remembered Loup winning the championship in 1936, he was standing there in the club.

He had told Rosaleen, his daughter-in-law, if Loup could ever win another one, he could die a happy man. Joe was taking it all in and shook my hand. He didn't say anything and I suppose he didn't need to. He was trying to hide it and you could see the tears tripping down his cheeks.

I remember meeting Paul McVey, who later won a championship in 2009, coming running on the pitch that day as a supporter with a headband and a flag. Then you had youngsters of three, four or five years of age, and it was great seeing what the joy did for them.

ULSTER WAS BONUS territory and I really enjoyed playing in the games. I wasn't as nervous, like in the Derry Championship. We just loved going to training with the feeling of being county champions. There was no pressure, but Malachy saw there was a chance.

We beat Bryansford by a point and everyone was writing us off for the semi-final with Crossmaglen. Going into that game, it wasn't as if we were saying that we'd definitely beat them, but we believed we could. That was huge, because if you'd told anyone that 12 months earlier, that we'd be at that stage, people would've laughed at you. Once we beat them, there was the realisation that we could win it and thankfully we beat St Gall's in the Ulster final.

We went on to win the Derry title in 2009, but in '05 when we got to the final under O'Rourke, and Bellaghy beat us fair and square on the day… that was the most disappointing day of our careers. I was really poor that day and, as a team, we totally underperformed, yet still could've won it. We still believed we had the talent there and '09, in our eyes, probably makes up for '05 in a way that you could retire content, not always happy, but content that you got that second one that you deserved.

KEVIN McCLOY

DUBLIN 0-18 ★ DERRY 0-15
All-Ireland SFC Quarter-Final
Croke Park, Dublin
AUGUST 11, 2007

★ **DUBLIN:** S Cluxton; D Henry, R McConnell, P Griffin; P Casey, B Cullen, B Cahill; S Ryan, C Whelan; C Moran (0-1), J Sherlock (0-2), B Brogan (0-3); A Brogan (0-3), C Keaney (0-3), M Vaughan (0-6). **Subs:** K Bonner for B Brogan, D Magee for Ryan, J Magee for Moran, T Quinn for Keaney.

★ **DERRY:** B Gillis; M McGoldrick, **K McCloy**, G O'Kane; K McGuckin, SM Lockhart, F McEldowney; F Doherty (0-1), J Conway; M Lynch, P Murphy (0-2), E Muldoon; C Devlin (0-2), Paddy Bradley (0-6), C Gilligan (0-3). **Subs:** E Bradley (0-1) for Murphy, B McGoldrick for Lynch, R Wilkinson for McEldowney, Patsy Bradley for Conway, J Diver for Gilligan.

66

PADDY CROZIER WAS in with Lavey when we got to the 1998 county final under Henry Downey as player-manager. Paddy suggested I should go to the Derry under-21s, but I didn't think I was good enough. I had never made the minor panel, but he planted the seed in my head and, next thing, I was up in Owenbeg.

I blended in fairly well and was at full-back on that under-21 team. We beat a good Tyrone team and Armagh that year, but we got beaten by a strong Monaghan side. I thought we could've done a bit better, but it probably gave me the hunger to continue. The progression to the Derry senior football team was still away in the future, and hurling was still more attractive at that stage of my career.

I hadn't a lot of success in football. I came up through Lavey underage and we

THE ACTION

★★★★★

DERRY CAME ALMIGHTY close to beating the Dubs in a proper rollercoaster of a championship game before coming up short.

Close friends Kevin McCloy and Paddy Bradley, who were both later selected in the All Star team, were Man of the Match contenders in an encounter that had a bit of everything. Fergal Doherty poured out every ounce of energy he had to try and claw Derry into the last four, but it wasn't enough.

Paul Murphy took two fine points in the first-half, before there was only deemed to be 35 minutes in a troublesome knee and he was replaced. The lead changed a handful of times in the opening half, with Bernard Brogan lighting up the early stages. Derry were within the kick of a ball at the break but needed a full-length Barry Gillis save to deny Brogan early on.

Paddy Bradley was on fire in attack, giving both Ross McConnell and Paul Griffin bother, but it was Stephen Cluxton, who saved twice from Eoin Bradley, who kept Derry at bay.

Dublin were seven clear with 10 minutes to go, before Doherty dragged Derry off the canvas and within three points. Their last throw of the dice saw a half-goal chance stopped by Barry Cahill's block, before Cluxton snapped up the loose ball and Dublin held on.

★★★★★

were short in numbers. All we won was an under-16 B league, but we went on to win a minor hurling championship and also the Ulster title. Winning was more attractive than getting beat in underage football all the way through my career.

I played minor, under-21 and senior hurling for Derry. We won Ulster senior in 2000, and were unlucky not to beat Offaly in the All-Ireland quarter-final that year. That was my first time playing in Croke Park. I was in my early twenties and quite in awe. I ended up marking Brian Whelahan for the last bit of the game.

My call for the footballers came the next year. Eamonn Coleman had been watching a game in Lavey and called me over. He told me Derry needed a full-back and asked if would I come up the road to Derry training. He also enquired if I was going to keep at the hurling, but I didn't, it would've been tough going to keep at both.

I had a lot of time and respect for Eamonn. He was a great people person. Whenever you get the call from a man of that calibre and from what he did for Derry before, you jump at the chance to play for that team with the fantastic players on it.

To come in out of the blue with very little experience at that level, I suppose I just threw the shackles off. I thought, *I am not going to get many chances…* that's the way I felt, so I had to take it when it came. If I am being brutally honest, I struggled in the first few games with the pace of the game and the cuteness of the full-forwards with the tricks they had, and I had to adapt my game.

Eamonn said to me after training one night about needing to improve my turn if I was going to play inter-county football. Night after night, Eamonn got me to stand with my back to him. He'd shout, 'TURN'… and would've been firing balls at me, left and right.

I thought I looked like a right prat in front of the rest of the players, but if Eamonn feels you need to improve on something and he is going to give you the opportunity, then, you are going to go with it. To be fair, I believed he was right and I was slow to turn, so it was a part of my game I had to work on.

It was the same with my kicking, I struggled at that high level. I looked at the players there. Paul McFlynn, Johnny McBride, Paddy Bradley, Enda Muldoon… players I felt I couldn't have laced their boots, and Anthony Tohill was still there. I was looking on in awe at a lot of these players.

I was marking Kieran Close on my championship debut in 2001 against Antrim and was taken off at half-time, so it wasn't a great start. I didn't play against Tyrone in the semi-final with an 'An Other' listed in the team, so I rang Eamonn to ask him where I stood? He told me just to be ready whether I was playing or not.

I felt I needed to know if I was playing, as it's a different mindset, but I didn't get a look in that day and we lost to Tyrone. We met Antrim in the qualifiers and I only got into the team because Sean Marty Lockhart was sick... and I didn't make the same mistake with Close the second time.

We went on a run that included a rematch with Tyrone, which we won to set up a semi-final with Galway. There was a lot of talk that week of who was going to mark Padraic Joyce. A lot of the talk was that it would be Sean Marty, but Damian Cassidy took me aside to tell me I would be on Joyce. I was told in the hotel the day before the game and maybe that was a ploy on Coleman's part, not to give me much time to ponder on it. As a young player, you might have thought too much about it but I took the chance with open arms. I wasn't one of these players who did a lot of analysing of opponents. I looked at their dummies, but some players will analyse them to the last.

I was a player who went on instinct and one of my best attributes was in reading the ball. I didn't see Joyce as any great threat, but if you mark the two Bradleys at training every night, the left footers don't tend to trouble you as much.

I thought I had a good day on him and Joyce didn't score from play off me, but the outcome was a downer after that game. To know a game was in your grasp and you could've been walking out there onto the red carpet on All-Ireland final day, that took a long time to get over.

Coming into the last 10 minutes, myself, Gareth Doherty and Sean Marty were saying about staying tight and keeping the goals out. Matthew Clancy scored the winning goal and I always think of how I should've come across the square. Joyce was standing in the six-yard box and if I left him, all he would've had to have done would be palm it in. But those are the choices you have to make in life.

It was just surreal; it was my first year in and I thought we were going to win the All-Ireland every year. As a young player coming into the panel, to reach an All-Ireland semi-final and to keep Joyce scoreless was a dream for me and helped cement a place in the team. We reached an All-Ireland semi-final in 2004. I missed it with a broken cheekbone but I remember us keeping it tight until half-time, until Kerry then took control.

Tyrone lifted Sam the following year, but we knocked them out of Ulster in 2006 and held them scoreless from play for the entire first-half in their own backyard. To beat the All-Ireland champions was something that Derry team needed, it gave us a bit of a lift.

WE LOST THE Ulster semi-final in 2007. I marked Tommy Freeman fairly well that day in Casement, but they were building into the team they became. We were expected to beat them and it really hurt. Monaghan had never beaten us in a big game before that. We drew Armagh in the qualifiers and beating them in Clones that day was a change in the season, but it wasn't on its own. We had three games in three weeks during July, with the wins bringing confidence back into the team.

I was captain against Armagh because Kevin McGuckin was injured. I remember saying that we should throw the shackles off because we had nothing to lose. Nobody in Derry expected us to win and, to be truthful, we weren't expecting to win ourselves because Armagh still had a good team.

I was marking Oisin McConville, and Paddy said if I could keep him out of the game it would go a long way to us winning… and I was Man of the Match that day. We were in control at half-time and let them back into it, but everybody put their shoulder to the wheel. We had more than Armagh in the last 10 minutes and Collie Devlin's winning point finished it off.

We beat Mayo easily the following week, when I picked up an injury that should've ended my season. I went down to block Conor Mortimer and when he took the shot, he followed through into my hand and broke my small finger. I thought it was dislocated, so I pulled it back out to where it should've been.

I was marking Barry Moran and when you are marking high-profile players, you grow in confidence a bit every day. I thought I had a fairly good game against Barry and we went in hot favourites against Laois the following week, but that's when Derry could sometimes lie down. We took care of Laois very comfortably and were back on track, on our way to Croke Park for one of the biggest games of my career, in a full stadium against the Dubs.

While I played in the Laois game, I had a fair idea there was something seriously wrong. The hand had swollen all week in training, but I didn't go to the hospital in case there would be bad news. I couldn't stick the pain after the Laois game, and went to Enniskillen hospital. The nurse asked me if I thought the injury was going to fix itself and they sent me straight to Altnagelvin. From there, they sent me home to fast, before coming back the next morning for an operation.

Two more weeks and the finger would've fused in the wrong place… it was broken in seven or eight different places. I went under the knife to get the finger reconstructed, with two pins and four screws. The knuckle was all smashed up into my hand, and the surgeon told me the hand was a lot worse. I saw the x-ray and it was bad. If we were to get to the All-Ireland final, they told me I wouldn't have been playing in that either.

Talk about being deflated, lying there on a bed with the anaesthetic wearing off. I couldn't believe it and I knew I wasn't going to get many more chances like this to play against Dublin in a full house. For the surgeon to tell me I wouldn't be playing, that was just devastating.

I rang Paddy Crozier to tell him the news, but he told me to keep it to myself and we'd never know what would happen before the game. We devised a plan that we'd go up to Musgrave Park hospital. Before I went, I cut off the Plaster of Paris and they made a special cast for the finger itself. The stitches weren't going to come out until two days before the game, and we needed a makeshift glove. We cut the finger out of the glove, put on the cast and taped another glove finger over it.

There was still doubt over me in the hotel in Castleknock on the morning of the game. Myself and Paul Murphy did a fitness test out in the car-park, but I couldn't catch the ball with the pain. I took painkillers to get me through the first 15 or 20 minutes, because when you get into a game and adrenaline starts… then the pain goes away.

They were kicking balls between me and Paul Murphy, and I told him to stay back for one so I could catch it without any punching. Once I caught the first one and came down without any excruciating pain I said, 'Paddy, I'm good'… and that was it. I was playing. I went into the hotel and made a beeline for the painkillers and there was no looking back.

On the bus to Croke Park, I was sitting there wondering if I had made the right decision. People were saying if I had a good game, then I was in line for an All Star. All sorts of thoughts were going through my head. It was a long road in, holding my hand and it throbbing.

THE MOST SURREAL feeling was running out to that full crowd in Croke Park with the hairs going up on the back of your neck. When you are in that cauldron, it is very hard to keep focused for the first 10 or 15 minutes, and it almost takes over your whole body. Before long, a game can slip past you if you get too involved in what's going on around you.

You have to put it to the back of your mind, but I have to say it was one of the best football or hurling experiences I ever had. I don't know where Paddy Crozier gets all his inside information from, but he had me on Conal Keaney that day knowing the Dubs would take me out around the middle with him.

I was to float about and it would suit me. I did relatively well on Conal, but there were a few big clashes that put me on the way to getting Man of the Match that day. There was the crunching tackle on Mark Vaughan. He had gone past Kevin McGuckin and Sean Marty. The Dubs were three or four up and if it had hit the net, the game was over. I had to leave Keaney and make my way across to him.

That tackle nearly put me out for a year and a half. I ripped nearly every muscle from my shoulder down into my groin. It was one of those tackles that, if I had lay down, I was going to look very bad with Vaughan lying in along the ball-catcher nets at the Canal End. I'd say that tackle won me my All Star, if I am honest.

EVERYBODY TALKS ABOUT that shoulder on Vaughan, but there was also a clinical one in the first-half, when Barry Cahill came down the middle. I hit him down the middle and the ball bobbled up from the tackle. It was nearly a sending off offence, never mind a booking, and the ball landed in my hands.

It was one of those days… every time I moved, the ball seemed to come to me so maybe someone was looking down on me. Looking at how I played, I always felt that reading the game was one of my best attributes and getting to the ball before the forward. I excelled when I could put a forward on the back-foot straightaway.

That day, there were a few occasions when myself and Conal slid along the ground and I came out on top, thankfully. The pace of the game was electric, it was end-to-end stuff and compared to the way the game is played today, we were very open at the back. They probably got their scores a lot easier than we did. We worked hard, if you look at some of the scores Paul Murphy, Paddy and Collie Devlin took that day.

I still wonder why Paul was taken off, but we can't change history now. He was one of the men that stuck out as having a good game until he was taken off. We were managing okay, but in hindsight we stood off them a bit too much and showed them too much respect. Quality forwards who get quality ball are always going to be hard to stop.

We had two goal chances that we missed in the second-half. If we had got one of them, even if we'd clipped them over the bar… we could've stayed in touch. The Dubs would be going into the last quarter under pressure, but they always seemed to have that comfort blanket to manage the game out.

I thought when a lot of our lads were out on their feet in the second-half, Fergal Doherty dragged us through the last 15 minutes singlehanded and I thought he was Man of the Match that day, if I am brutally honest. It was one of the best midfield performances I ever saw, but it was a disappointing defeat.

In 2001, getting to the cusp of an All-Ireland was a bit of a surprise and we were there before we realised it. In '07, we knew we had a decent team and had built well through the backdoor in July. We believed we could beat Dublin. If a couple of the goal chances had gone in, we'd have been sitting against a Kerry team I wouldn't have feared. Looking at the semi-final and how they beat Cork so convincingly in the final, it was a chance we threw away.

I WAS NOMINATED for an All Star in 2005 and felt I should've got one, but getting Man of the Match on a losing team against the Dubs was a help in getting nominated in '07. In the weeks coming up to the selection, the word on the street was how Paddy Bradley had been nominated five times and, having a fairly decent year, then he was going to have to get one.

My thinking was that there wouldn't have been room for beaten quarter-finalists to get two. Paddy wasn't going to go down, if he wasn't getting one, so he made a few phone calls to check it out… as it was a year when the football awards were announced on the night.

I was in Enniskillen working when Paddy rang me to say he was going, so I congratulated him on his All Star. At that point, I thought that was me out but he told me I was going to have to go too, and that was his way of telling me I got one.

I packed up early from work and went home to get ready for going down to Dublin, so it was a great drive home that day. Paddy was a few years younger than me, but when I joined the Derry panel, we just hit it off and we'd often travel to training together. To get the award with him, of all the players I played with, made it that extra bit special. If anyone deserved one from those 12 or 13 years of playing for Derry, it was definitely Paddy.

PADDY BRADLEY

GLENULLIN 0-10 ★ BELLAGHY 1-6

Derry SFC Final Replay

Celtic Park, Derry

OCTOBER 21, 2007

★ **GLENULLIN:** S O'Kane; E O'Kane, Brian Mullan (0-1), Barry Mullan; S Mullan, J O'Kane, G O'Kane; R Boylan (0-1), N Mullan; D McIlvar (0-1), D Boylan (0-1), C Bradley; D Hasson, **P Bradley (0-4)**, E Bradley (0-2). **Subs:** B Rafferty for Hasson, D McNicholl for S Mullan, D Higgins for McIlvar.

★ **BELLAGHY:** M O'Neill; M McGoldrick, M McShane, K Doherty; E Scullion, C McNally, P Diamond; F Doherty (0-1), J Diver; R McNally (0-1), G Doherty, G Diamond; D Graffin, R Rocks (0-1), E Brown (1-2). **Subs:** C Brown (0-1) for G Doherty, S McNally for McShane, K McLarnon for Graffin, C Murray for Rocks.

WHEN I WAS in with Glenullin seniors at the start, in the early 90s, we took some bad beatings against the so-called stronger teams. We had our fair share of bad days, sandwiched in between some decent championship performances.

I was on the panel in 1997... I was 15 or 16 at the time, when we took Dungiven to a replay and they went on to win Ulster. We should've beat them both days and had the reputation at that time for being able to put it up to anyone on any one day.

Were we championship contenders?

No way.

After that, there was a period of four or five years when we had a relegation play-off to hang on to our Division One status. At that time, we'd have gone to Ballinderry or Bellaghy and been beat by 20 or 30 points. We started to compete

THE ACTION

★★★★★

GLENULLIN BRIDGED A 22-year gap to win their third Derry SFC title, with Paddy Bradley kicking the winner two days after picking up an All Star award.

As in the drawn game, Glenullin got the better start and were 0-4 to 0-1 ahead at the end of the opening quarter, with Donal Boylan, Paddy and Eoin Bradley (two) hitting scores after Ryan McNally opened the account for the Tones.

A Ruairi Boylan point looked like it would give the Glen a three-point lead with half-time approaching, only for a palmed Eoghan Brown goal getting Bellaghy back into the game against a dominant Glenullin side, who finished with 17 wides in total.

Bellaghy manager, Damian Cassidy, hatched a game-plan of sitting Eugene Scullion in front of Paddy Bradley, but the game changed on two fronts. A second booking for Kevin Doherty had Bellaghy down to 14 men. The other factor was how Brian Mullan and Gerard O'Kane bossed the game from the half-back line.

Dominic McIlvar, and Paddy Bradley from a free, levelled the score by the midpoint of the half before Eoghan Brown edged Bellaghy back in front. Brian Mullan sliced over a fine score to tie the game again. Paddy Bradley and Fergal Doherty – who was also nominated for an All Star – exchanged scores, before Bradley won the title with a late point from a tight angle.

★★★★★

regularly and move higher up the table, however, and we started to win James O'Hagan Cups and Dr Kerlin Cups on a regular basis.

To people on the outside, it may not seem like a big deal, but to us it was, because it got us into that winning habit. We won the Ulster League in 2007 and that was the catalyst. It was a significant enough competition, a lot of the best teams in Ulster were playing... and we ended up winning four Ulster leagues.

That year we beat Latton down in Emyvale, when we came from maybe three or four down to win it, and that gave us serious belief. Things snowballed that year and everything seemed to go right for us, even in the games where we were playing bad we got into the habit of digging out results.

The belief started to build from the two or three years previous, because we were competing with the bigger teams. We were no longer getting beat out the gate. We might've lost the game, but you were thinking to yourself you are not that far away.

In 2005, we were beaten in the semi-final by Loup and we probably should've won that game. I should've been given a free with the last kick of the game, a decision that didn't go down too well. We missed chance after chance on a really wet day, and put Loup to the pin of their collar and they'd won Ulster two years earlier.

If you look at the team in 2007, it had a good mix of younger and older players. I had been playing regular football for the seniors for quite a few years before that. You had Dominic McIlvar and Brian Mullan, who had been in and around the Derry senior panel. Eoin (Bradley) and Gerard O'Kane... Eunan and John O'Kane had experience of underage county football. You had Damian Hasson, who was getting on in years but was a very intelligent footballer with experience of playing with Derry. Ruairi Boylan, another experienced man... there were very few men on the team who didn't play county football at some stage. We felt that our team was as good as anything in Derry.

Even going to the Kilmacud Sevens... we were able to compete in semi-finals, semi-finals and finals. We knew we had a core of players that were as good as there was about the country. Da (Liam) had been drilling it into me and Eoin for 20 or 30 years. Going across the road from Kilrea every night for training, he was constantly telling us, from when we were no age, we'd win a championship.

We are a generational club. Da's team won it in 1985 and there is a generation lost that went to America and different places, so they should've won more. It was the sons of many of those men that were the next batch of players to win it.

You looked at your players against the other teams in Derry, with da constantly driving the thing on. Chairman Martin Mullan had a committee and whatever was needed, was met; they were phenomenal. You need that bit of luck too; we won that championship in 2007 and we had luck, whereas in other years we passed up two or three championships.

THE LEAGUE TOOK care of itself in 2007. Even without me, Eoin, Gerard, Brian and whoever was away with Derry, we were picking up enough points. That was a good sign that even without a couple of county men, we can still compete and it showed us how strong we were getting.

Da put a serious emphasis on reserve football and we were able to play 15-a-side games in training, with six or seven men waiting in the wings every night. When I came on the panel, there were 20 or 21 men training and you were gathering men from their beds with a hangover on a Sunday morning to fulfil a reserve fixture.

We got through the group stages and even in the quarter-final against Magherafelt, although we didn't play particularly well, again that was a sign we had arrived because we never looked in any bother.

The big one was the semi-final with Ballinderry, down in Bellaghy, and it was probably my best ever game in a Glenullin jersey. I think I kicked nine or 10 points. Anything I hit seemed to go over and I was marking Kevin McGuckin, a good friend. That was the first time we had beaten Ballinderry in a meaningful championship game in so many years, and they were the standard-bearers.

Nobody gave us a chance that day, but we wiped the floor with them. Donal Boylan was exceptional that day, Conrad Bradley at wing-forward... to a man, each and every one of us stood up. There were only two or three points in that game, but, truthfully, we won that game comfortably.

To put it in context, we played them in an under-14 Féile semi-final in Greenlough and Eoin was doing nets. I had been our main player at the time... they beat us by 40 or 50 points. I am not joking you. I'd say they hit 13 or 14 goals that day. We played them in an under-16 final and it was the same thing... I got sent off that day, and they maybe beat us by 25 points, and then we met them two years later in minors and beat them.

It wasn't the exact same team but it was a core of the same players and it showed you the development that was happening in four or five years.

I remember getting a 14-yard free and roofing it. I remember Cathal Óg Mullan making six or seven one-on-one saves. Ballinderry were the better team, but we hung on and got the result.

It gave that group of players great belief and the nucleus of those teams played in that senior semi-final in 2007.

I remember it being said in the changing room before that '07 senior game, the talk about the development from under-14, to under-16 and minor, and that it was the day to make the statement.

There was euphoria and we had a good drink in the club to celebrate it, but the focus soon turned to Bellaghy, who with Ballinderry, were also the standard-bearers.

It wasn't as if you had played the final in the semi-final. We knew how difficult Bellaghy were going to be and we knew about the number of titles they had and how used they were playing in finals. We knew we were underdogs again, even though we had beaten the favourites.

WE WERE LUCKY against Bellaghy in the drawn final. We didn't play well and they missed a chance to win it.

It was our first county final in a long time and there was serious euphoria around the community. There were cars painted green and yellow, goats painted green and yellow... there wasn't a road that didn't have a flag on each post. Looking back on it, players let that get into their psyche a bit. It is important that you enjoy the build-up to a county final, especially when it is your one and only or the first in a good few years, but we probably didn't detach ourselves enough from it.

More and more people started to come and watch training, and all of a sudden there could've been 12, 13 or 14 boys watching you train and wanting to know what was going on? Things got a bit loose, management tried to guard against it but it's hard for the mind not to wander and think *what if.*

We had watched a motivational video. Da had been videoing training sessions all year... sessions at the beach, at the forest and matches. He put a montage together, and Dermot McNicholl came in and talked to us before the drawn game. There was stuff in the paper and people were reading that, there were the predictions from all the experts.

On the Sunday morning, there was a big send off from the club. None of that happened the second day, things were much calmer.

The first day, we were worrying about tracksuits with county final written on them. We were eating in the Beech Hill Hotel in Derry on the way home. There was none of that the second day. There was food in the club. There was no send off, and Gerard O'Kane senior threw a horseshoe into the bus for luck as it was going out the gate.

I HAD THE All Star do on the Friday night in Dublin, but I wasn't going down after all the years of not getting one. One of the selectors had heard this and a message was sent to me via another man that I needed to be in Dublin, so it was obvious that I was getting one.

Myself and big Fergal (Doherty) were at the do together and were playing against each other on the Sunday, so we were both sober and up the road for training the next day. I never really got to celebrate it, but there was a double celebration after the championship win.

There was pressure on to perform on me and Michael McGoldrick was a brilliant marker. He marked me very well both days, but Damian Cassidy had a good system in place and they did a number on me.

Most of my scores against Ballinderry came down the left side, for a left footer coming in on the right side and curling in. I was sort of coming in on my unpreferred side.

I remember Damian, a few years later when he was the Derry manager, down in Laois before a league game, boasting about 2007 and how I didn't get a kick over the two games. I was well marked and he talked about watching the Ballinderry game closely, and blocking the channel I made my runs in. Kevin Doherty marked Eoin, Michael McGoldrick marked me very well, but Cookie (Eugene) Scullion sat in front of me the whole time and I struggled to get into the games.

I joked that as well as they marked me, I still kicked the winning score. The winning score came from kicking from a really tight angle on the left side with my left foot. I had worked and worked on that. For years and years, it was something I did. I worked on kicking across the body from tighter angles.

To be the one to kick the winning score was fantastic, with all the years of practising from that side of the field. When you look at it, I was probably mad to take the shot on. It was a narrow angle, only eight or nine yards off the end-line.

One thing I never suffered from was self-doubt when I was going to take a shot. At Ireland training, they called me 'Paddy Angles'... the tighter the angle the better chance I have of scoring it. Before training starts, people are kicking from tight angles so I had never any bother taking those shots on. Particularly in the dying embers of a game and you know it is a 'shot to nothing', with a chance to win a county title... and to see it sailing over the bar was unreal.

We watched that replayed final one night in the club a few years ago and I forgot how dominant we were. We missed chance after chance, and I missed simple free-kicks; some of the shots we had dropped short but, thankfully, things came up trumps for us. I will take being marked out of the game two days in a row, even if it wasn't me that kicked the winner.

All the years of training, and all the years of work that started at under-8 and under-10 with da... him and Basil Rafferty took most of our underage, and it was all about winning a senior championship.

While we dominated that game, it sort of changed with a few switches. Gerard O'Kane was well marshalled in the first game and he was a very pivotal player for us from wing half-back. The second day, da moved John O'Kane out to wing back and put Gerard to the centre, meaning he was harder to pen in. That had a big input and, as that game went on, Brian Mullan, who had played full-back by default, was moved out to wing back... so we had Gerard and Brian launching every attack.

As that game went on, eventually we smothered Bellaghy. We were winning every ball around the middle of the field and those two boys were running and kicking ball... that was the platform for winning the game. It looked like we had eighty percent of the ball, but we couldn't get the scores and there was a nervousness there, probably from not winning a county title before.

AT THE TIME, Gerard O'Kane Snr had a watch with a Glenullin and Derry crest on it. At the final whistle he hit it against the wire or the dugout, and the pin came out. It fell off and he hasn't worn a watch in his life since. Time stood still. It's the wee things that show what it means to people.

I was captain for a period of six or seven years, and Brian Mullan was appointed captain when I was away with Derry. We got into the habit of getting Brian up lifting the cup with me.

We were very good friends and it was a good memory of us lifting the cup together… and Gerard won Player of the Match that day. There is a good picture of the three of us.

The cup was carried into the hall that night by daddy and Martin Mullan. It was magical stuff. With the crowd of people that night, that never leaves you. To have the community out… to a man, woman and child, and to bring something back to your club like that, that's what all the sacrifice and training was for.

I am so relieved for da and Martin Mullan, for all the underage managers and managers that took teams. They had put so much effort in and look where the club has come under Martin's chairmanship, with the facilities… he had the utmost belief in that team. To see the joy on those boys' faces!

But we partied too hard. There is not a day goes by I don't regret that group not winning a second championship or going deep into Ulster, because I felt we had the team to do it. Preparation-wise, it was our first county title and we probably thought we'd be back here again.

We never really treated it with the respect it deserved, and it is criminal to say that. We drank for nearly the full week… the bar lifted £17,000 over the two days and that showed you the level of celebrations. That would be double the money now.

We didn't draw a line, and I take a lot of responsibility for that. I was captain of the team and Wednesday should've been cut-off point, but we went to Maghera, Swatragh, the Port… we went to Belfast, it was a full week.

We beat Newtownbutler two weeks later, and were expected to beat them. We didn't suffer from the lack of preparation until we played St Gall's a few weeks later. They were a great side and beat us, but we didn't prepare properly.

The weekend before the game, boys were nipping away for a pint here and there. Nowadays would we be doing it? Probably not. There was the belief that we'd be here again, but it didn't happen. I am not saying we were as good as Slaughtneil or the current Glen team, but we didn't give ourselves the best chance to go on and perform in Ulster.

99

KEVIN McGUCKIN

BALLINDERRY 2-5 ★ KILREA O-6
Derry SFC Final
Celtic Park, Derry
OCTOBER 16, 2011

★ **BALLINDERRY:** M Conlan; D Bell, **Kevin McGuckin**, C Wilkinson; M McIver, C Nevin, R Scott; Kevin 'Moss' McGuckin, M Harney (O-1); D Conway, R Wilkinson (2-O), T Martin; R Bell (O-1), E Muldoon, C Gilligan (O-3). Subs: A Devlin for Martin, D McGuckin for D Conway, N McCusker for Bell, R Wilson for McIver.

★ **KILREA:** P Morgan; J Darragh, A Rainey, M McWilliams; B Óg McAlary, L Morrow, J Morgan; C Kielt (O-1), James Kielt (O-1); E Morgan, J Donaghy (O-1), E McAleese (O-1); G McWilliams, B Quigg (O-1), P McNeill. Subs: P McAlary for E Morgan, T Rafferty (O-1) for G McWilliams, D Johnston for McNeill, E Darragh for Quigg, Jack Kielt for J Morgan.

66

SOME OF MY earliest football memories are going to Derry matches. I have a memory of sitting in the old wooden seats in Clones for a Derry and Tyrone match on a scorching day. There is photo of myself, mammy, daddy and my brother, Stephen.

I remember sitting in the Pat McGrane Stand for the Ulster final against Donegal in '93, with the water running down off the hill behind us. There was also the famous Dublin win in the All-Ireland semi-final that year, when daddy had us sitting in deadly seats in the upper Hogan Stand. I can also remember my da doing goals in his last year for Ballinderry, being well into his 40s at that stage. And I remember going to matches all around the country – in our house the weekends were just for going to football.

THE ACTION

★★★★★

TWO EARLY GOALS from Raymond Wilkinson and a solid platform saw Ballinderry climb back to the top of the tree again in Derry. After losing to Coleraine 12 months earlier in the decider, the Shamrocks bounced back to take the title for a first time in three seasons.

It was a proud Kevin McGuckin who raised the John McLaughlin Cup aloft 30 years after his father, Pat was the winning Ballinderry captain.

Kilrea were newcomers to county final day and they were rocked after a mere 43 seconds. A long, wind-assisted ball from Man of the Match Martin Harney found Enda Muldoon who teed up Wilkinson for his first goal, squeezing his shot past goalkeeper Paul Morgan from the acutest of angles.

Ryan Bell and Harney hit points, before Ballinderry struck for their second goal. Conleith Gilligan sliced a free into Muldoon at full-forward and, seconds later, Wilkinson blasted to the roof of the net.

James Kielt, Enda McAleese and Benny Quigg were on target for Kilrea, who trailed 2-2 to 0-3 at the break. Facing the breeze in the second-half, Muldoon played at midfield and three points from Gilligan kept the scoreboard ticking over. Kilrea had a goal chance in the closing minutes, but Denver Johnston was denied by Michael Conlan... and John McLaughlin was back on his way to the loughshore.

★★★★★

For my own football, with Ballinderry, the training was different to what you have now. Now you have so many underage teams, from the under-6s and primary school football, all the way up. Back in the late 80s and early 90s football only started at under-12 with a few P7 matches at primary school.

At that time, daddy took the under-12s and because he was the manager, I'd have been down around at the pitch since I was eight or nine years of age, stuck in the training with the older boys. I wasn't overly mad about football when I was very young, it was only when I was in P6 or P7 that it really clicked with me.

We had a decent school team and we played over at the Maghera Tournament. I remember we had a tough semi-final against a Terry McFlynn led Swatragh team and I was marking Paula McAtamney. She was an unreal footballer and gave me a bit of a toasting. We played Glenview in the final, and Antoin Moran was that age and we'd some great tussles over the years.

At that time, in our house, there were no trips away to Spain. If you got to the All-Ireland Féile, that was your summer holiday and, luckily enough, we got to a few. As youngsters, you didn't know where you were going and the Ballinderry community all really bought into it. Literally, it was the whole of Ballinderry on tour and was a special time.

We went to Navan one year and the whole of Ballinderry had caravans and camper vans. We took over Navan O'Mahony's grounds. A big memory back then would be Joey Mullan. He'd have been famous for having the craic on those weekends, singing in the bar. He'd a song *Shaving Cream*, and he'd be singing away… it could last three minutes, five minutes or 10 minutes. As a young fella, those were great memories as all our friends would've been down.

On one of the years when I was playing, 1993, we were hosted by Kilcummin in Kerry and I rooming with my good friend, Conleith Gilligan. It's amazing how a family of strangers would take you in for the weekend, feed you and drive you to all the games.

It was a special competition.

THE ONE THING about daddy, he was always happy to tell you how good he was. He played full-back and he'd have been hitting the kick-outs… and he'd have taken the 45s as well. He has a rugby background as well and if he was watching a game or seeing people kicking 45s, he'd be telling you how good of a place-kicker he was. I don't have a lot of actual visual memories of him playing, but I vividly remember him as a coach.

Nowadays, once you become a father, you have to muck in and become one of the coaches. That naturally happens with small community clubs likes our own, but daddy stayed with the under-12s every year, regardless if I was there, Stephen, or whoever was involved.

Then you had Kevin Collins with the under-14s and those were the stepping stones to taking players through the ranks. That's not easily done year after year by the coaches but that was the structure they had. Fair play to them.

In 2002, when we won the All-Ireland club, I had just turned 21 in February. I probably got lucky enough breaking in. Coming up through the ranks I wouldn't have been a corner-back as such, I was more of a half-back or a midfielder on the underage teams I played on.

I was more of a No 6, but when you are breaking into a senior team that has Ronan McGuckin wearing No 6 and Niall McCusker at No 3, then you are just looking for any place at all. On that team, we'd Paul Wilson on one wing and Darren Crozier on the left, so breaking in there was tough. I was a big skinny drink of water. It's not like now with boys coming in having done their gym work. Our preparations would've been all fitness-based back then, with running to build up the legs.

One of my very first games for Ballinderry, we were playing Slaughtneil and I was marking Padraig McKaigue, now my brother-in-law, who was corner-forward and I didn't know who he was.

The year of the All-Ireland, I was battling with Shane Mullan for a corner-back spot. There would probably have been three solid, pacy, young corner-backs at that time… myself, Shane and Jarlath Bell. That was fortunate for the team because we were pushing each other hard but it was unlucky for Shane as he got squeezed out.

Once I slipped into the team, then thankfully, I was able to lock that down at age 21 and I held a spot in that full-back line for years.

IN BALLINDERRY, WE went through a serious spell of success when we had a lot of quality players and everybody bought in. When it came to weddings, holidays and even opportunities of going to play football in America, everybody just put the club first.

There was a serious emphasis on winning championships. At that stage, club football was so competitive. When I look back now, the club did get the full focus, possibly to the detriment of the county. We would have had a county game on a Sunday and would maybe have played a league match on the Monday night – probably not ideal. But the boys involved loved the club and wouldn't have missed a training night, never mind a match.

It is great to see the success of Derry at the minute, with the players putting the county first. Back then, the clubs possibly got all the emphasis and Derry were playing second fiddle a bit, and that's unfortunate because we had so much quality on the Derry panel at that time. Those Derry teams could've done more, but we didn't because there were so many passionate club men throughout all the clubs.

At that time, around the 2010 final, Ballinderry had maybe taken a bit of a dip and were possibly aging a bit and losing a couple of players. Coleraine were a good team, and mobile. They brought a different brand of football to it and losing to them in 2010 was a tough one to take. We had sneaked through the semi-final with Lavey that year, with late goals. It was a 'smash and grab' that day down in Greenlough, so maybe we weren't really at that level to win the championship.

Coming into 2011, there would've been a bit of pressure and I don't know if the level of expectation was the same as in previous years. As players, we knew we were hungry and we all wanted it. Martin McKinless was back over the team and there was no shortage of desire being driven in the group. We were training on our bottom pitch and in the dark. There were 100 and 200-metre runs, it was a really tough grind. It wasn't always enjoyable but there was a big push on to get to where we needed to be.

The focus of that tough training was a bit of both building fitness and character. When you think about camaraderie, spirit and coming together as a unit, nothing builds it like working hard together.

The Coleraine defeat was a really bad one. It was maybe seen as one that got away, a real gunk, or maybe it was seen that we were not the kingpins anymore. There were a lot of questions asked after that year. It is like any defeat you have; you'll ask the questions. Were they fit enough? Was there enough in the legs? Did they want it enough?

Martin came in, and he was looking to build it up and raise the bar again. He is a massive man for fitness and hard work and passion. You can have all the talent, and thankfully we did have it, but you need to have the hunger, desire and belief to get it across the line.

It's funny when you look back on it. That was the first year of a three in-a-row, but that year, in that moment, the question was about seeing if we could get back to the top table. Never in a million years would we have been dreaming of three in-a-row at that point. We were asking if we still had it? Obviously, with winning the championship again, we proved we could and everybody bought in.

We had a mix; there were the older experienced players, but we had youth coming through at that time. Ryan Bell as corner-forward breaking through that year was still a very young lad. We had Aaron Devlin and Tony Martin putting pressure on starters. Darren Lawn was coming through. Then we had boys who had played a lot of football, but weren't overly old.

It was about getting going again to see if we could compete and, thankfully, that set the ball rolling. When we got the first title, we kept it going to get three, and an Ulster club, so it was a very successful period for us… where at the start of it, we weren't one hundred percent sure, or our supporters weren't sure, if we were still up to it.

MARTIN MADE ME captain for 2011, and it wasn't always the case that someone playing county football is the club captain because you'd want him to be there all the time. The mad man that I was, when I was made captain I was there all the time and took great pride in being named captain.

When you are a young fella, you dream of lifting the John McLaughlin Cup and being the man at the top of the steps lifting it on behalf of your team and parish. I was captain in '05, but we had a rough semi-final defeat against Loup that year. We lost by two points with a late goal and it was a year when we were ripping it up. We had won the league and everybody was sharp.

When we were nipped in the semi-final, I thought, for me, that's my opportunity gone to be a winning captain, with the names and the number of leaders we had. I clearly remember phoning Deirdre that night from outside the Bridge Bar, and it was a real low point. I had thought I had blown a great chance and, to be fair, we really did that year with the team we had.

When Martin pulled me aside to tell me they were making me captain, in 2011, it was a serious boost for me and an opportunity to give it a push. And I did that. I was still playing for the county at that stage, I was giving the club and county absolutely everything, and thankfully all the hard work paid off for us. That's the thing, everybody did buy into it and Martin always wants one hundred percent and he totally got it in 2011 and the years after it.

We beat Dungiven in the semi-final that year, with wins over Lavey and Bellaghy. We also had beat Kilrea in the earlier rounds before they came through the backdoor with a quarter-final win over Slaughtneil on the way to the final. It was a tough campaign, coming up against all the top teams, so it was definitely a nice one to come through.

In the semi-final, a big memory is when Aaron Devlin went down and we had a bit of a scare on the pitch for a few minutes, but he was okay, thankfully, and was then available again for the final against Kilrea. We felt a bit of pressure going into that final because of the 2010 defeat and, while we had got back to the final, nothing would mean more than winning it.

We were still tasting the hurt from 2010 and there is no worse feeling than the journey home from Celtic Park after losing a county final, and we didn't want a repeat of it. I felt a bit of pressure, but it didn't come from daddy, because he would never have wanted to put any pressure on me. There was a bit of talk around the club of it being 30 years since he had lifted the cup as captain in 1981.

It wasn't on my radar that much. I never bought into it or looked too far ahead, but you would think about it. Not only for us to win… but it would be something special for me.

We were coming up against a Kilrea team who were strong and we had real battles with before. We knew it wasn't going to be easy. I would've known the Kielt boys and Brian Óg McAlary through county football, and I'd have got on well with those lads. We knew we were going into a real cracker of a game. For any county final, you know you have to be on song.

Martin liked to have four big men across the middle of his teams. We had been playing with Mossy (Kevin Moss McGuckin) and (Martin) Harney in the middle. Then we had two big wing half-forwards. Enda (Muldoon) would've pulled out around there too.

Martin McKinless had Dessie Ryan involved in the management too. Himself and Dessie were massive fans of the high ball. You want a couple of Endas… one kicking the ball in, and one catching it inside.

One thing we worked on was the long ball… Dessie used to talk about the trajectory of a pass in. He was famous for asking us to try one at the end of a session. If worked, brilliant, but if it didn't, you could be trying it for 20 or 25 minutes.

Ryan Bell was new to the scene and he'd be in under the high ball with myself or big Niall McCusker marking him. Then, if it didn't stick or he wasn't in the right place, Dessie would say, 'Let's try that one more time'… and that could've gone on for a while. For a young fella, that wasn't easy but that's what Dessie's planning was all about.

It was about getting it right… what side the ball breaks to and who it breaks to. There was meticulous planning in it. Sometimes, a big ball lumped in can look like a Garryowen but, with us, there was definitely more to it than that. Martin Harney was a great man to deliver a ball. Darren Conway, Crook (Raymond Wilkinson), Collie Dubh (Devlin) or Deets (Conleith Gilligan) if he wasn't playing inside. One thing we did have were super kickers.

There were a couple of big long balls planted in that day against Kilrea and they did damage for our goals in the first-half.

Coming up to that game, there was pressure and expectation as there is of every Ballinderry team in a final. There is nothing we wanted more than to win. There were nerves… there always are. Martin would be a very passionate speaker. The changing room was brilliant and we were up for it.

A memory I have of the game was early on. I think they won the first ball and I was playing at full-back on Benny Quigg, who had scored the winning goal against Slaughtneil.

Kilrea got a ball around the middle and pumped into our defence at the Brandywell end. It was one of those, as a full-back, where you are thinking about it being the first ball of the game and asking yourself if you were making it. *Do I go for it? Or do I stay with my man?*

James Kielt was chasing towards it and I was in the full-back line. I thought, *I'll take a chance on this one…* and it was a race between me and James, with the ball in the middle. Thankfully, I got to the ball, had a crack off him, but came out with the ball. I remember thinking it was a good start. If I hadn't got to it, it would've left Benny free in the square… so it was one I needed to get. It settled me down and set a bit of a tone.

It wasn't a very high scoring game, but we got those two early goals and were well set up. It was a slog, a defensive one, and we certainly worked for it, but it was just great to get over the line.

WHENEVER THE FINAL whistle goes, it turns into complete bedlam. You don't know who is hugging or beating at you. For me, to be the privileged man to lift the cup, there was nothing like it. I was going around trying to find the family, to find Deirdre and to see where everybody was at.

Then, it's funny. After a while, it settled, until my da landed in. He'd never watch any of the games. He'd be outside the grounds and somebody would be keeping him up to date. I don't think he saw a ball kicked that day, but I'd say he has watched the video a number of times. I remember him coming onto the pitch, and meeting him in the goalmouth down at the changing room end. It was pure emotion.

We have a lovely photo in the kitchen in the home house of him lifting the cup in 1981, of me lifting it 30 years later, and us embracing after that final. They are super and privileged memories. That day in Celtic Park, I remember going up the steps, and the buzz and the personal thing of me being the one to lift the cup. From such a group of men, for me to get that honour, it meant so much to me.

I hadn't really prepared a speech. You have daydreams about what you are going to say. I hadn't written anything out, but I remember loving what I said.

I said it wasn't just for the players, this is for everybody… supporters, the community and people who weren't there. I remember the roar that went up after that. It was a contrast to 12 months earlier. Declan Bell had picked up an injury early on against Coleraine. I had punctured a lung in a challenge game and was just back in for that final, so I wasn't fully fit. The feeling on the bus on the way home in 2010… it was about where we were going to go from there.

The following year, you are going down the road and there are a few bottles of beer floating about on the bus and a sing song. There was a great mix of us, the more mature players, and the young boys who had broken through… and those tough wins just bonded us all together for life.

CHRISSY McKAIGUE

SLAUGHTNEIL 0-12 ★ ST VINCENT'S 0-10

All-Ireland Club SFC Semi-Final

Páirc Esler, Newry

FEBRUARY 11, 2017

★ **SLAUGHTNEIL:** A McMullan; F McEldowney, B Rogers, K McKaigue; P McNeill, **C McKaigue (0-4)**, K Feeney; Patsy Bradley, P Cassidy; Shane McGuigan (0-3), Paul Bradley (0-2), M McGrath; C Bradley (0-3), Sé McGuigan, C O'Doherty. **Subs:** R Bradley for Sé McGuigan, B McGuigan for K McKaigue.

★ **ST VINCENT'S:** M Savage; M Concarr, J Curley, C Wilson; B Egan, G Brennan, Cameron Diamond; N Mullins (0-1), S Carthy (0-1); G Burke (0-2), D Connolly (0-1), Cormac Diamond; R Trainor, E Varley (0-5), T Quinn. **Subs:** A Martin for Trainor, J Feeney for Cormac Diamond, K Golden for Cameron Diamond, F Breathnach for Mullins, S McCusker for Egan.

66

NOBODY IN THEIR wildest dreams would've dreamt of Mickey Moran coming in to manage us. The appointment came as a shock and it was equally as big a shock that Mickey Moran was interested in the job, being from Glen and well through his managerial career at that stage too.

I heard a club member asked him of his interest and he said he'd be very interested, so it was put forward through the process. As far as I know, there wasn't too many in for the job. It was a shock to most of us and you'd have been in dreamland if you'd have predicted how it would've gone.

You need the boys who are 30, or approaching 30… you need the middle boys who are in their physical prime, the 24 to 27 or 28 bracket… then you need the raw freshness, naivety at times, to gel everything together.

THE ACTION

★★★★★

HAMMER THE HAMMER. How often have you heard that phrase when going head-to-head with a key opponent? Slaughtneil's passage to a second All-Ireland final was the perfect example, as Chrissy McKaigue went toe-to-toe with Diarmuid Connolly and came out as the undisputed winner with four points from play.

The Emmet's needed a late Paul Bradley insurance point and a fully-stretched Antóin McMullan to claw Shane Carthy's flick out of the net. But the performance was led by McKaigue taking on one of the game's greatest artists and painting his own masterpiece.

After coming through the preliminary round to win a second Ulster title, Slaughtneil arrived in Newry for a David vs Goliath encounter, a rural superclub against one of the urban superpowers.

Christopher Bradley scored the opening point for Slaughtneil after four minutes, but Vincent's had a good first quarter and led by 0-3 to 0-1, before the Ulster champions' defence began to take root. St Vincent's led 0-6 to 0-5 at the break before Slaughtneil and McKaigue turned up the heat further.

It was the third quarter that laid the platform for victory, with McKaigue (2), Christopher Bradley and Shane McGuigan all finding their range. Vincent's go-to men were being bottled up by Slaughtneil's well-drilled defence and McMullan's save kept the Dubs at bay.

★★★★★

There is no doubt we had that in abundance in 2014, but it was amazing at how it developed and became more structured and more tailored towards the model we wanted to go for.

The 2014 season was not a perfect year for us in many ways. There were ups and downs, the championship was far from free-flowing. We had a stinker against Dungiven and I always use that example of knockout football, but we showed our class in the replay when our heads were switched on and won that game really, really comfortably.

The Ballinderry game gets the headlines for obvious reasons, the last-minute goal and if it was over the line? When you look back on that game and, even Ballinderry people say this, if we'd lost it, it would've been a travesty.

We controlled the game and had several chances. We definitely did enough to win the game and we proved that by our passage through Ulster, and then we proved it again in the years after.

The reality is that if 2014 doesn't happen, it's a game-changer. The goal was the biggie, but I remember looking around at the frustration during the game at the chances we were messing up. I remember scoring the point before half-time. I vividly remember Adrian McGuckin saying to us around team talks, the psychological difference of going in at half-time four points down or three points down is huge. That was in the back of my mind when I attacked that last ball before the interval… we needed to bring it to a three-point game.

Ballinderry were very happy with their half's work and we got it to three just in time. Ballinderry beat us plenty of days when we weren't the better team, but if they had beaten us that day it would've been us *losing* it rather than them *winning* it.

When you look at it logically, when you look at Mickey Moran's personality, when you look at the difference in our team, the level of performance in 2014 and '15, to '16 and '17, it was chalk and cheese. The team was always going to develop and it probably coincided with the fact that Ballinderry weren't coming to the fore like they were in their earlier years and we were the new kids on the block.

Between 2016 and '17, we were winning most Derry championship games by an average of seven-plus points.

WHEN YOU WIN your first provincial crown, there is the surreal moment and you can't believe it has just happened. With the next one, there is never the same euphoria after it and I remember after we had beaten Kilcoo in '16, there was an unbelievable degree of satisfaction that we had got back. I remember it not being as euphoric, but there was the satisfaction. Then, I remember Keelan Feeney and a few of the young boys chanting a song about us going to Wembley. When we got to the meal, I honestly knew nothing about it and people were talking about us playing the London champions, St Kiernan's.

I didn't believe how that would be possible. All I remember that in '16, I couldn't wait to get a break. I was mentally struggling. Thomas Cassidy passed away, there was the schedule of football and hurling week in and week out. It was borderline too much for me in terms of the pressure of being the first club to have won the first Ulster hurling and football titles.

I went into that Kilcoo game thinking, *We just need to get through today…* it was like a dagger into my heart to realise we were going to London two weeks later and the razzmatazz attached to that. For me, all I could think about was the fear of getting beat. I have never been as terrified of a game in all my life, and that's the honest truth.

To think we had come through eight games in 10 weeks, and it takes its toll. I was extremely resentful of these boys getting to play in an All-Ireland quarter-final after us coming through Ulster; they should've at least gone into a provincial series first, like it happens now.

There was nothing to be gained for us, it was a distraction and I can remember everybody around the club gathering money. It increased my worry with supporters going over and this carnival-like atmosphere. I remember thinking we could get our eye wiped here. There was a lack of focus and I remember Mickey Moran being the same.

There was fear of failure and the embarrassment of getting beat. I wanted to get back into an All-Ireland semi-final again. I was never as driven or as motivated to get us over the line. In the hotel that night before the game, some of our players had a jovial atmosphere and I snapped at them, and Mickey Moran snapping at them pretty viciously too.

From the moment we left the runway in Belfast, until we went to bed in London, there was a distraction in our group, an immaturity among our younger players. It was the depths of Christmas and there were parties going on in our hotel. It was not an atmosphere conducive to an All-Ireland quarter final.

Mickey was always more worried about the so-called smaller ties in Derry and Ulster than he was with the biggest games. He never worried about Slaughtneil on the biggest days, because he knew we would be focussed. He worried about us on the smaller days. It shows his humility and professionalism, and never taking anything for granted.

I remember watching the St Vincent's Leinster final when I got home that night and the commentator saying that surely the match-up in the semi-final would be myself and Connolly. I was thinking this would be the narrative that would dominate. Coming home on the plane, I breathed a sigh of relief… I wasn't going to go near football or hurling for a number of weeks.

I had been around the county scene for a while and had made a good enough name for myself at that stage for marking key players. It became the narrative but not as set in stone as it was for others that I'd pick up Connolly.

MICKEY TREATED EVERY opposition the same. I vividly remember the meeting before we played Newbridge earlier in Mickey's tenure and he knew the name of Newbridge's last sub as well as he knew the name of Ballinderry's star forward. I never saw a man that made it his business and his pride to know every single player in the opposition, who they were and what they were about. There was never a bad word, and very few managers have that.

Usually, you go into a dressing-room and you hear negative things of the opponents. Mickey Moran built up the opposition, sometimes too much, but his psyche was very clear – you have got to prepare for the best of any opponent. There was no way that approach could fail and Connolly was no different. Give people the full respect, but the best person to respect is yourself and your own teammates.

I remember the St Vincent's game being shown on the big screen in the clubhouse in London; it was in Tullamore against Rhode and they won quite comprehensively. St Vincent's had huge pedigree, but the tie gained the most razzmatazz because of Connolly and about what he was doing in the county game. He was the poster boy of the GAA and I remember seeing montages of Connolly's best scores on Facebook and Twitter. Even the buzz around the club and the young ones, they couldn't believe we were going to play Diarmuid Connolly's team.

At underage level, I would've scored a fair bit, but that St Vincent's game was different because of the magnitude of it. In an under-21 final for Derry, I scored two points from play and won another free and that was as close to it.

To caveat that, for the vast majority of my career, certainly at inter-county level, I have been playing in the full-back line. For Slaughtneil it is 50-50, but for Derry I have been in the full-back line. I had a real lease of life playing for Slaughtneil because I wasn't playing in the full-back line, and I was enjoying that so much.

My position has depended on the level of football. At county level it is a stopper and I have excelled at that role. At county level it is harder to attack with the way I play it. In club football, sadly, with the years going by, it's as an organiser more than bomber and an attacker.

It's an evolution of where you are. One example I use is Ryan Giggs. You can have longevity if you are humble and smart enough. I can change my role and accept what I can't do anymore because, unfortunately, age catches everyone.

It was a long-standing conversation at the time about where I'd play against St Vincent's, because a lot of teams, during Mickey Moran's reign in Derry and Ulster, would push a man to No 11 to man-mark me. We knew that wasn't going to be the case against St Vincent's, but we weren't against that idea because you just never know.

It wasn't talked about at all and there was a long lead-in coming up to that game. I can honestly say, and that was the beauty of Mickey Moran, we went overboard on the way the opposition played and gave them respect, but we never went overboard in terms of personnel no matter how big a star they had in their ranks. That was the same with Diarmuid Connolly, it was very, very simple. It wasn't really discussed until we played St Vincent's on a Saturday, and we had a meeting two days before the game.

We knew on the Thursday evening that I was on Connolly. We would've decided who we'd mark, along with Mickey, and that was the beauty of our dynamic. He was very much the man who made the final call, but he listened to what we had to say.

It wasn't rigid. We knew from the videos that there were times against Rhode that he went to midfield, and there were times he went to full-forward and on those occasions I wasn't to follow him. Mickey Moran was a great advocate for not changing his own team, which showed the faith he had in us. It's documented Connolly scored a point, but I wasn't on him for that play, Brendan was on him.

One of the points I scored in the first-half, he wasn't on me either. I was on him for the vast majority of the game, but for the last 16 or 17 minutes of the first-half and the second-half we did mark each other. A lot has been made out of the Diarmuid Connolly tussle but for the most of my Derry career, from when I came back to Ireland in 2012, I was marking the marquee players across Ireland.

One of my first games back at full-back, I marked Stephen O'Neill against Tyrone and throughout that whole year I marked some big players in the championship, culminating with Michael Murphy in the championship in Ballybofey. I have been lucky to have a few good marking displays. One that stands out in the back of my mind, that is never mentioned, was on James O'Donoghue and he talked about it on *The Football Pod*.

I marked him in 2014 down in Killarney. He was at the peak of his powers then in a league game. He scored 1-3, or something ridiculous, in the game prior to that. Nobody really knew who he was and I remember seeing the clips of him and thinking, *I don't really want to mark this man. He is gold dust.*

He was ripping it up and I held him well, and that is one that stands out in the back of my mind. There wouldn't have been 1,000 people at the game. Derry were in Division One at that stage, so it wasn't brand new, but it was Connolly who had superstar status from who he was, what Dublin were doing and the way he played the game.

For me, it wasn't any different to how I prepared for any of the other ones. To my mind, a marquee player was a marquee player. I remember going in a point down at half time and being relatively happy. We knew it would come down to fine margins anyway. I remember the feeling on the pitch that day, it is there for the winning… there was no mad sense of we can't believe this is happening.

I have never saw a competition like the All-Ireland and Ulster club, where experience means so much, even to this day. The experience we have as a club and players to have played on those occasions.

I remember the second-half and being in a really good position of being a point down… and going a couple up. We were in a position of control. Antóin, our goalkeeper, made a massive save from a fairly fortuitous flick, but he was on guard. In the last five, six or seven minutes, like any big game, there were a few nerves to get over the line and with that, St Vincent's threw the kitchen sink at it.

A massive turning point in that game was when their goalkeeper came out and took too much out of the ball and… bang, a scoreable free.

I remember looking at that free and thinking to myself, there was nobody else I would've wanted to have the ball but Paul Bradley. It wasn't a gimme, but the way he struck it, it wasn't looping over the bar or skimming the post, it was struck true and over the middle spot. After that, our name was on it.

WE WERE CONVINCED we were going to win the All-Ireland.

What people tend to forget is that great Corofin team were beaten that weekend by Dr Crokes by nine points, hammered. Crokes beat us at the peak of their powers and we were at the peak of our powers. It was fine margins. People do Crokes a disservice of how good they were.

People say about Slaughtneil leaving it behind them; getting a man sent off and all those things. When you look at history books, Crokes absolutely dominated Munster that year, hammered everybody, and hammered Corofin in the semi-final.

Us and them came down to the finest of margins, two club teams in Ireland at the absolute peak of their powers.

99